A WIDOW'S MIGHT

My Story

(or more accurately)

HIStory

By

Hope D. Lundy

This book is dedicated to:

Jesus: my Savior, King, and soon to come heavenly husband. God the Father, the Ancient of Days. The Holy Spirit who's my comforter, teacher, standby and dearest friend. My late husband, Danny Lundy, who's walking the streets of gold and watching from the banisters of heaven. My family, friends and ministry partners who've been praying and extending the love of God to us in so many unexpected and beautiful ways.

I also want to personally thank my pastors, Drs. Rodney & Adonica Howard-Browne for boldly standing and preaching the undiluted Gospel and always challenging us to come up higher. Words can't express what your ministry has meant to me and the eternal impact it has already had on our family. The fire you carry and give to others not only set my late husband free but is fueling my launch into ministry around the world, to the glory of King Jesus!

Table of Contents

Welcome   7

Chapter One: In the Beginning   13

Chapter Two: A Solid Foundation   22

Chapter Three: Expectations & Disappointments   32

Chapter Four: God's Way   44

Chapter Five: Talk to Him   57

Chapter Six: Praise Is a Weapon   71

Chapter Seven: Healthy Boundaries   83

Chapter Eight: Guard Your Heart   103

Chapter Nine: Father Knows Best   116

Chapter Ten: Holy Spirit & Fire   130

Letter From the Author   144

Biography   145

About The Author   146

WELCOME

Congratulations on taking important steps toward learning to fight well for your marriage, family, friends, and to rise into your own God-given destiny. When the Lord had me write this book, He had you on His heart. He's seen all that's happened, He's heard your hearts cry and He's even caught every single tear you've ever cried.

His plan was never for us to merely get by or white knuckle it until He comes back to get us. Now, He is coming back soon, for a glorious church, one without spot or wrinkle. And He wants His people to learn the authority that we've been given and to really rise into the fullness of all Jesus died to make available to us, this side of heaven.

You don't have to settle for less than what the Bible says you can have. You really can have a wonderful marriage; you can live a life full of abundance, supernatural faith and joy and really step into ALL God has in His heart for your life. In Jeremiah 29:11 it says, *"For I know the thoughts and plans I have for you, says the Lord, thoughts and plans for welfare and peace and not for evil, to give you hope in your final outcome"*. God has good things for you and the only way to actually discover them is to walk and talk with Him daily

& allow Him to lead the way into a future that is far greater than you've even dared to imagine.

Just to settle the record up front... God does NOT place sickness on His kids to teach them a lesson. The enemy comes to steal kill and destroy according to John 10:10. God will use things that happen and work them out for our good and we should be learning valuable lessons along the way. But sickness, death and poverty are from the devil. He is the one that wants to steal, kill, and destroy, not God. Would you as an earthly parent use a known abuser to punish your kids? Would you throw your kids out in traffic to teach them about the dangers of crossing the road without you? NO, of course not. So why do we sometimes blame God in that way? Why do we attribute things to Him that we, as less than perfect parents, wouldn't even do? It all boils down to really getting to know Him. When we come to know His character and begin to really walk with Him daily, in personal relationship, we discover He's a good, good Father. A far better parent than we are, and His greatest desire is to bless His kids.

What better place to deal with wrong views, bitterness, or anger towards the One who loves you than right here, right now? If you've had a wrong understanding of God, been holding onto past hurts or offense, or perhaps you've not been walking with Him like you know you should, it's time to get it right. So why not just take a moment and talk to your Father, repent if needed and decide, right now, to give Him unrestricted access to every area of your life? A pure and open relationship with the Lord is the only true way to find fulfillment and lasting joy. He really is the way, the truth, and the life. If that relationship isn't right, the others have no real hope of working either.

If God is not your Father and you've never accepted Jesus as your personal Lord and Savior, we must address that first. None of what I'm sharing in this book will work for you until you take that crucial first step. Maybe you love the Lord, but you've gone astray, and He isn't Lord of your life anymore, your love has grown cold. It's time to get right with The King so you can really discover what He has for you. Romans 3:23 says, *"For all have sinned, and come short of the glory of God.."*. Romans 6:23 says, *"For the wages of sin is death; but the gift of God is eternal life through Jesus Christ our Lord."* And Romans 10:9 says, *"If you confess with your mouth the Lord Jesus and believe in your heart that God has raised Him from the dead, you will be saved"*.

So right now, out loud and from your heart say "Dear Lord Jesus, forgive me of my sins and wash me clean. Come and be my

Lord and my Savior. I believe You are the Son of God, you died, and rose from the grave and You're coming back for me. Help me to live for You. Give me a hunger for the things of God, a passion for the lost and a holy boldness to preach The Gospel of Jesus Christ. I'm saved, I'm forgiven and I'm on my way to heaven because I have Jesus in my heart."

As a minister of the Gospel, I declare to you that if you said that out loud and believed it with your heart, YOU ARE SAVED!!! All your sins were completely forgiven and all of heaven is rejoicing over you right now!! Always run to God and never from Him because He loves you so very much!

Just a few things to help you on your journey… read your Bible every day, preferably the King James (KJV), Amplified Classic (AMPC) or New Living Translation (NLT). (Steer clear of the NIV as they have altered much of the Word and it's not accurate, especially the newer editions.) You can also download an app. called YOUVERSION from the play store to try the different versions and even listen to the Bible audibly. I use it a lot when I'm driving or busy working on something. A great place to start is the book of John. You'll learn about Jesus and the covenant you are now privileged to be under. Talk to your Father all throughout the day. He LOVES to hear from His kids. Prayerfully get plugged in to a local church. One where Jesus is truly Lord and the Word of God is honored, boldly preached and undiluted and where the Spirit of God is free to do as He sees fit.

The Spirit of God, the Holy Spirit, longs to teach you, heal you, and lead you into sure victory. (You can read more about Him in the book of Acts, as well as all throughout the Bible.) But He won't force you to follow or step into what He has for you. He is however beaconing you to come, taste and see all He has in His heart for you. In John 10:27 it says, *"My sheep hear My voice; I know them, and they follow Me".* God really does talk to His people, if you're wrestling with hearing Him don't worry, we'll be diving into that soon, but it all begins with true surrender. And a willingness to really listen.

The very definition of insanity is doing what we've always done and expecting different results. If we truly want change, real, lasting change, we must be willing to embrace change, ourselves. It is my prayer and belief that this book will encourage, embolden, and challenge you in ways that, if you're ready and willing to grow with God and partner with the Holy Spirit, it will alter the trajectory of your personal walk, your marriage, and your family. You can be the one God uses to alter your family legacy; and you will see the fulfillment of the deepest desires of your heart and your God given destiny as you give The King your lavish YES!

To God be ALL the glory, honor, and praise!

Chapter 1

In the beginning....

It was February 2, 2002, around 5am, when I had my encounter with Jesus that would prove to change EVERYTHING I was, all I thought I knew and all I wanted in life. Jesus has a way of doing that and I'm so very grateful! My life was a complete mess when the King walked right in. He wasn't afraid to come and sit with me. He wasn't put off by the worldly stench that surrounded my life. He climbed right down into that pit I found myself in and rescued me, from me.

You see, I was working the overnight shift at the Ford plant in Kansas City, Missouri, and while I was making good money, I wasn't making good choices. I'd gotten heavy into smoking pot, drinking, and partying on a regular basis. Most days I was high all day long, trying to run from the deep-rooted pain I felt from a life steeped in sin.

That fateful morning, I had come home from work, per the norm, showered and smoked a joint to wind down. I started to feel really sick. I heard a voice that said, "get in the shower, you'll feel better". I thought, "that's the dumbest thing I've ever heard. I already took a shower." I recall trying all I could to feel better with the typical crackers, water, trying to get sick, etc. But nothing worked. I heard the voice again, "get in the shower, you'll feel better". At a point of desperation and feeling like I would die, I relented and got in the shower.

I wasn't even able to adjust the water temperature before I was on my knees with my life playing before me like a movie reel. I saw, in color, all my sinful ways, and all the ways my choices were keeping me away from a Holy God. And for the first time in my life, I encountered the lavish love of God Almighty. I came face to face with the reality that it was never His will to be far from me, but it was my choices that were creating the distance.

I had accepted Jesus as a little girl but the Father, He was different. To me Jesus was love but the Father was ready to smack me with His sovereign rod for the mess I'd made of my life, and boy did I deserve it. My wrong understanding of God the Father caused me to keep Him at arm's length and run my life "my way". And I suffered many things in life, not because God brought them upon me or caused them to happen, but because I had chosen a life outside of

His covering. Outside of a relationship with the One who loves me, and you, in ways that no human ever could.

I repented in that shower and asked God to forgive me. I was weeping from the depths of my being & longing to be fully embraced by the love I was encountering. As the water cascaded down my tear-streaked face, I heard Him say, "I wash you white as snow". I was saved!! I was forgiven and my feet were placed on a path that would lead to an eternity in the presence of the Almighty God. Halleluiah!

I became ravenously hungry for the Word of God. I would read it day and night. On the assembly line I would read between working on cars and the Lord became one of my dearest and only friends. Most everyone I had called friend previously, abandoned me. They enjoyed spending time with the partier but this godly woman I was transforming into, they didn't know how to handle her. I left work crying most days after being ridiculed and mocked, feeling very alone. But I was growing strong on the inside and I kept devouring the Word. I eventually started a Bible Study on lunch break that a few came to. It was nice to have a little community there.

After much prayer I got moved over to 1-line. Few people over there knew me which was a nice change. I could focus on my work and the Word and didn't get much pushback. That was where Danny and I had our first real conversations. Within a short period of time, we'd developed an unexpected friendship and he got saved at a Carmen concert we went to with some friends. When I gave my life to the Lord, I took a vow of celibacy and vowed not to date until He showed me the one.

Our friendship was growing, he came to help me move into my house, we went to church together or hung out with friends but tried to be careful to maintain healthy boundaries. That can be pretty tough when you haven't really known healthy boundaries, especially in personal relationships. I recall fumbling my way through those days resisting my default tendencies and leaning into God's will. I didn't do things perfectly but boy was my heart set on trying to do it right.

It was in that season that I really began to hear the voice of God. Sometimes we have to be stripped free of all the outside noise to tune in to the One that really matters. I was eating the Word like my life depended on it. Little did I know I was being transformed on the inside by the *"washing of the Word"* (Eph. 5:26). As I read, God was cleansing me from the inside out. You see, many people have this misconception that they must "get their act together" before they can come to God, but the truth of the matter is, He's the One that does the cleaning and transforming. We can't do it on our own if we could Jesus wouldn't have had to die in our place.

Many people also believe that once they say the "sinner's prayer" they have fire insurance to keep them out of hell and they can live however they want. That couldn't be further from the truth either. Jesus must be Lord of our life. Heaven forbid we take for granted the price He paid for our entrance into His family, the New Covenant and our promised eternity with Him.

One question we must wrestle with is how do we show love to someone who so lavishly loves us? What's the proper response? Humanly speaking when someone loves us or goes out of their way for us it becomes our desire to reciprocate. Shouldn't that be our natural response, and all the more, with Jesus? *"We love Him, because He first loved us.",* 1 John 4:19. You may be asking why I'm even going here but I submit to you that love must be our motive in all we do.

We won't be able to fight for our marriages and families without love, the God kind of love and we won't see our world changed without love. 1 John 4:8 says, *" He who does not love does not know God, for God is love"*. It's His love and His presence that will enable us to fight well, to love well and to step into victory in every area of life. The God kind of love empowers us to fulfill what 1 Corinthians 13:4-8 says, *"Love endures long and is patient and kind; love never is envious nor boils over with jealousy, is not boastful or vainglorious, does not display itself haughtily. It is not conceited (arrogant and inflated with pride); it is not rude (unmannerly) and does not act unbecomingly.*

Love (God's love in us) does not insist on its own rights or its own way, for it is not self-seeking; it is not touchy or fretful or resentful; it takes no account of the evil done to it [it pays no attention to a suffered wrong]. It does not rejoice at injustice and unrighteousness but rejoices when right and truth prevail.

Love bears up under anything and everything that comes, is ever ready to believe the best of every person, its hopes are fadeless under all circumstances, and it endures everything [without weakening]. Love never fails [never fades out or becomes obsolete or comes to an end]."

Looking back at all the years between then and now one thing I wish I would've done differently is to have prayed and declared 1 Corinthians 13:4-8 over my marriage and family from day one. Which is exactly what I'm doing now pertaining to my family, myself, and my future marriage. There're so many scriptures about the importance of what we speak and what we believe. The Word of God gives us firm footing and even if our reality doesn't look like what it says yet, we can stand on the Word and declare it until we have what God says we can have.

One thing we all discover on this walk with the Lord is that when we desire a change in our situation, marriage, family, or anything really, the transformation first starts with us. And if we're willing to align with His will then we really can have heaven on earth as Jesus taught us to pray in Matthew 6:9-13. *"After this manner therefore pray ye: Our Father which art in heaven, Hallowed be thy name. Thy kingdom come, Thy will be done in earth, as it is in heaven. Give us this day our daily bread. And forgive us our debts, as we forgive our debtors. And lead us not into temptation, but deliver us from evil: For thine is the kingdom, and the power, and the glory, forever. Amen."*

Key Takeaways

- Nothing is impossible with God!!

- We must feed on the Word of God.

- We can bring our mess to the Lord, and He will do the miraculous.

Declarations:

❖ According to 1 Corinthians 13:4-8, Because God is love and He lives in me, I walk in love that endures long and is patient and kind; my love is never envious and doesn't boil over with jealousy, it's not boastful or vainglorious, it does not display itself haughtily. It is not conceited; it's not rude, and it doesn't act unbecomingly.

❖ My love does not insist on its own rights or its own way, for it is not self-seeking; it is not touchy or fretful or resentful; it takes no account of the evil done to it. It does not rejoice at injustice and unrighteousness but rejoices when right and truth prevail. My love bears up under anything and everything that comes, is ever ready to believe the best of every person, its hopes are fadeless under all circumstances, and it endures everything [without weakening]. The God love in me never fails. Amen!

Chapter 2

A Solid Foundation

" Therefore whosoever heareth these sayings of mine, and doeth them, I will liken him unto a wise man, which built his house upon a rock: And the rain descended, and the floods came, and the winds blew, and beat upon that house; and it fell not: for it was founded upon a rock. And everyone that heareth these sayings of mine, and doeth them not, shall be likened unto a foolish man, which built his house upon the sand: And the rain descended, and the floods came, and the winds blew, and beat upon that house; and it fell: and great was the fall of it." Matthew 7:24-27

We were just two twenty-somethings in love with the idea of love, dreaming of a house filled with laughter, love, and beautiful babies. When we first started talking, I could tell that we were in different places, but I believed since he'd accepted Jesus as Lord that we were "equally yoked". Boy was I wrong. Being equally yoked actually means Jesus is Lord of both of your lives and you're walking together in the same direction that He's set before you, at the same pace. If you're not married and you see red flags here in your personal relationship, WAIT! If you are married and unequally yoked, pray, trust God and don't give up on your Covenant. God will take care of you, your marriage, and your family if you stay faithful.

We got married on June 15, 2002, and that started a whirlwind of challenges, joys, and sorrows as well as unmet expectations, on both of our parts. God's timing can be trusted and looking back, I'd say we got out ahead of His plans and purposes. Had we deferred to His ways and His timing we could've overcome many challenges individually, before we got married, and our marriage would've proven much different, no doubt.

Over the next several years I discovered the importance of being rooted and grounded in The Word and allowing God to fulfill the deepest desires and longings of my heart. The importance of allowing Him to do whatever He saw fit with my husband, not trying to change him myself and allowing God to work on me personally. I came to realize that I had no say about how my husband would choose to live but I could make a difference for myself and our children. My times with the Lord, and in the Word, would become so precious to me that without them I likely wouldn't have made it through the many challenges that came.

We Must Build Our Lives Upon the Rock

One of the greatest principles we must learn in our walk with the Lord is the importance of getting into the Word and really allowing the Word to get into us. If you've never read through the entire Bible, I'd encourage you to start in the book of John and read on through Revelation then go back to Genesis and read through to the end. When I read the Bible, I usually ask the Holy Spirit to guide me and give me eyes to see and ears to hear and that He would give me revelation of the Word.

I'm not sure who to credit for it but I love the saying, "The Bible is the only book whose author is always present when you read it". Why not ask Him to be your guide as you open the Words He had penned? We should never read the Bible just to read it, it's not merely some book on a dusty old shelf. It's the Living Word of God. It's actually Jesus Himself according to John 1:1. Merely collecting a bunch of Bibles, but never actually reading them, doesn't work either. That would be like going to the gym, looking at the equipment, touching some of it and watching other people work out and expecting to get fit. It'd sure be nice if it worked like that, but it doesn't. We must work the Word.

James 1:22 says, *"But be ye doers of the word, and not hearers only, deceiving your own selves".* After we discover truths in the Word, we need to prayerfully reflect on that new knowledge we've received and ask the Lord to help us to become what it says we're to be and to do what it says to do.

One technique I've employed over the years is writing out the verses and posting them where I'll see them regularly. Then I read them out loud; sometimes as a prayer or declaration over myself, my family, situation, or over other people or things that are on my heart. Isaiah 55:11 says, *"So shall My word be that goes forth out of My mouth: it shall not return to Me void [without producing any effect, useless], but it shall accomplish that which I please and purpose, and it shall prosper in the thing for which I sent it."* You see we've been given the Word not just as a book we should feel obligated to read but as a change agent that can transform things in our day to day lives.

When my kids were little, I put post-it notes and index cards all over the house with scripture. If I was wrestling with fear, for instance, I would find scriptures that addressed fear, read, and memorize them until they got into my spirit and the fear broke. Again, John 1:1 says, *"In the beginning was the word and the word was with God and the word was God.*" Jesus is the Word on those pages. As we read, we become more acquainted with Him and His ways. And He becomes such a part of us that when we're squeezed Jesus comes out, or the Word comes out. Doesn't that sound much better than curse words or bad attitudes bubbling out? We can train ourselves to speak life instead of death. I've heard it said that the life we're currently living is a product of what we've spoken into being. Amen or ouch! May we be a people who choose the life-giving Words of God and reject the non-sense the world says is normal and acceptable.

We can learn to wield the Word and use it to bring about change in every area of life. Just pick an area in your life that doesn't line up with what you see in scripture, find a verse that speaks to that thing and start working the Word. (There're many tools and resources at our disposal today that make this practice super easy. Even a simple Google search will draw a ton of scriptures. Just check your Bible version and stay close to the original text)

Romans 4:17 tells us to call those things that be not, as though they are. So, what would you like to see change? Don't let yourself get overwhelmed by the big picture if there's several things out of line with scripture. Ask the Holy Spirit to show you where to start and start there. He's the One that brings forth the change as we yield to Him. When I got saved, I had this HUGE list of things I knew needed to change but as I stayed in the Word and walked it out with the Lord, I discovered His list was different from mine. His list addressed the root of the issues and not merely the symptoms.

He's into doing the deep, foundational work that's necessary for lasting and true change. After all, you can't build a solid house on a crooked foundation. I mean, you could try, and things would "look good" from the outside but when the storms of life come, they'd take your house out and expose the crooked foundation. It's much easier to let the Lord get right to the heart of the matter and show you how to create a foundation worth building on. He is after all the Master builder, and He can be fully trusted with even the most vulnerable parts of your being. Isn't it interesting to note that Jesus was a carpenter by trade in His human form? He's very skilled at building things even in the natural.

Some verses I've stood on for many years are:

To Counter Fear:

"For God hath not given us the spirit of fear; but of power, and of love, and of a sound mind." 1Timothy 1:7

For Salvation of family:

"...Believe in the Lord Jesus Christ [give yourself up to Him, take yourself out of your own keeping and entrust yourself into His keeping] and you will be saved, [and this applies both to] you and your household as well." Acts 16:31

Victory:

"And the Lord shall make you the head, and not the tail; and you shall be above only, and you shall not be beneath, if you heed the commandments of the Lord your God which I command you this day and are watchful to do them." Deuteronomy 28:13

Provision:

"Give, and [gifts] will be given to you; good measure, pressed down, shaken together, and running over, will they pour into [the pouch formed by] the bosom [of your robe and used as a bag]. For with the measure you deal out [with the measure you use when

you confer benefits on others], it will be measured back to you." Luke 6:38

The lasting impact of this practice won't be fully realized until we step into eternity, but I have seen SO MUCH happen because of it in every area of life. God has transformed me, my family, my finances, and more as I've prayed and declared scripture. If you employ this simple practice, His Word will not return void. You will see change and God will receive the glory!!! Our words are powerful, no doubt, but His Words...... Infinitely powerful!!!

We are transformed by the renewing of our minds through the washing of the Word. That's where we discover what good, noble, and holy things to set our attention on. The Word must become such a part of who we are that even if they took our Bibles, we could feed on what's inside of us until Jesus comes to get us.

Key Takeaways

- The foundation of our lives must be built on the Word.

- Memorize and declare scripture over every area of your life.

- Posting scripture and meditating on it daily gets the Word into us and brings forth change.

Declarations:

❖ According to Romans 12:2, I am not being conformed to this world, but I am being transformed by the renewing of my mind. And I will prove what is the good, acceptable, and perfect will of God.

("And be not conformed to this world: but be ye transformed by the renewing of your mind, that ye may prove what is that good, and acceptable, and perfect, will of God.")

❖ According to Isaiah 55:11, God's Word shall not return void, but it shall accomplish the perfect will of God in my life, marriage, and family. In Jesus name.

("So shall my word be that goeth forth out of my mouth: it shall not return unto me void, but it shall accomplish that which I please, and it shall prosper in the thing whereto I sent it.")

Chapter 3

Expectations and Disappointments

"Trust in the LORD with all thine heart; and lean not unto thine own understanding. In all thy ways acknowledge him, and he shall direct thy paths." Proverbs 3:5-6

When Jesus got ahold of me, He set my heart ablaze, and I started running with Him, I was ALL IN. Not everyone is ready or willing to do that. The Bible tells us not to be *"unequally yoked"* in 2 Corinthians 6:14 and many believe that's simply accepting Jesus as Lord, like I did. But it requires much more, especially within a marriage covenant. By definition: a yoke is a wooden cross piece that is fastened over the necks of two animals and attached to the plow or cart that they are to pull. Now if you yoke any two animals where one is way stronger than the other it could break the neck of the one of lesser strength, which could prove deadly. What if one ox chooses to go a different direction? Again... they aren't equally yoked.

Both people, of course, must first accept Jesus as Lord and Savior but both must also be willing to fully surrender to running the race He sets before them. This is essential to fulfill the plans God has for their marriage and family, pulling in the same direction, at the same pace, accomplishing the tasks at hand in unity. Thus, fulfilling the plans and purposes for which the Lord brought them together in the first place.

Knowing and employing this simple truth could save you many years and even a lifetime of heartache, frustration, and disappointment. In my own life, my late husband did not want to soar to the heights I felt drawn and called to, so I hit a ceiling in ministry. When two people get married they become one flesh and God is not going to raise one up into a position that will leave the other vulnerable or susceptible to falling. *"Can two walk together, except they be agreed?"* Amos 3:3 The answer is really no and no amount of desiring or hoping for it will change that.

Now prayer can absolutely change things, and nothing is too hard for God. But I've often wondered if we'd waited to get married if it would've changed things. Perhaps we could have worked through some things individually before becoming one and we could've avoided a whole mess of issues. Perhaps we'd have decided not to get married at all. Either way, I wish somebody would've told me then what I'm telling you now.

With that said, if you aren't married, be content in the waiting and trust His timing. God knows so much more than we do, and He can be fully trusted. If you find yourself unequally yoked, in marriage, don't give up or give in. Keep your spouse before the Lord and speak life. If I had it to do over, I would have celebrated the small wins so much more instead of being so focused on what was missing. In all honesty, I felt very alone for many, many, years of my marriage because of this very issue. When Jesus is your everything, being able to share what He's doing and showing you, as well as going before His throne together, becomes a huge desire of your heart. It can be very difficult not to be able to share the biggest part of your life with the one closest to you.

Sitting in church alone or with your kids and never feeling like you fit in can be very difficult and that certainly added to the loneliness I was feeling. I wasn't single but my husband wasn't really involved so that eliminated involvement in many groups and activities at the church. That can be a place where the enemy tries to make you feel ostracized but I'm here to encourage you, don't take that bait!! Stand strong and do what you know are the right things to do in in due season you shall reap a harvest!!

In different seasons of our marriage, I saw dramatic change and break through. As I let the Lord lead me, guard my heart and my mouth I would see vast improvement but when I leaned into my own understanding, things got messy. It may sound like a no-brainer to allow Jesus to take the lead but it's harder than it sounds sometimes, as some of you well know. It can be increasingly difficult when your other half is "popping holes in your boat" or doing things that are in direct opposition of the Word or how you desire to live. That's where we learn to really pick up our cross daily and die to self. That's when trusting the Lord becomes the lifeline that keeps our head above water.

One thing that's paramount when living an unequally yoked existence is that we cannot, under any circumstances, defy the Word of God and what we know is the right thing to do. For instance, if your spouse doesn't believe in tithing you still need to tithe. That can be tricky with people's varying financial situations but if you both work and they refuse to tithe, at least tithe on your pay. Some people get caught up on whether it's 10% based on gross or net but the real question is what part do you want protected?

Malachi 3:10-11 tells us to, *"Bring ye all the tithes into the storehouse, that there may be meat in mine house, and prove me now herewith, saith the LORD of hosts, if I will not open you the windows of heaven, and pour you out a blessing, that there shall not be room enough to receive it. And I will rebuke the devourer for your sakes, and he shall not destroy the fruits of your ground; neither shall your vine cast her fruit before the time in the field, saith the LORD of hosts."*

I don't know about you but personally, I want God to rebuke the devourer off ALL of my finances. And I have some big things in my heart to do for God that will require my finances to be blessed by Him. So, I make sure to not only tithe on the gross but to give abundant offerings above and beyond the tithe as well. You can't outgive God but it's sure fun to try.

You may be a stay-at-home mom thinking, "I don't have a job or any income that I can tithe off of". That's where you may need to get creative if your husband won't budge on tithing. The first thing we should always do if our spouse is in direct opposition to the Word of God is to go over their head and straight to The Father. No amount of us nagging, begging, or complaining usually makes much of a difference, in fact it often only causes greater discord in the home and robs the family of much needed peace.

But when we take our spouse, child or whoever before the Lord and release our right to be angry and offended we actually free-up God's hands to move on our behalf. As a stay-at-home mom you could have a garage sale of the things you don't use and tithe off that. If you bake something, why not give a tenth to your Pastor? If you have a garden, you could tithe off the harvest. God sees the heart and if we will be faithful with the little, He will bring the increase.

There were so many years that the financial numbers made no sense on paper but because we were faithful to tithe, the Lord was faithful to provide. Not that we never struggled financially but we never went without. Our kids were always fed, clothed and in a warm, comfortable home. God blessed the efforts of our hands and helped us to raise some beautiful babies. And to be candid, God was Father to our kids anywhere either of us lacked. I know Danny loved me and our children very much he just struggled to show it and because of my past I had challenges in loving him well too. Blending two lives takes work, commitment, and intentionality but if we're willing and we really allow God to be at the center, we will not fail.

Unfortunately, we live in a time where society and even many in the church view marriage as temporary and an easy thing to end but that's not what we see in the Word. The two become one according to scripture. Have you ever scrambled two eggs then tried to separate them back to their former state? Impossible!! So it is with marriage. Divorce is not God's will, and we must do whatever it takes to not only honor our marriage covenants but to love our spouses according to 1Corinthians 13. And yes.... even if they are difficult to live with.

1 Peter 3:1-5 says, *"Likewise, ye wives, be in subjection to your own husbands; that, if any obey not the word, they also may without the word be won by the conversation of the wives; While they behold your chaste conversation coupled with fear. Whose adorning let it not be that outward adorning of plaiting the hair, and of wearing of gold, or of putting on of apparel; But let it be the hidden man of the heart, in that which is not corruptible, even the ornament of a meek and quiet spirit, which is in the sight of God of great price. For after*

this manner in the old time the holy women also, who trusted in God, adorned themselves, being in subjection unto their own husbands…"

Now I'm not trying to imply that this is easy, but it is possible with the Lord. There's a grace that comes as our hearts are willing to obediently serve our husbands as unto Christ. Did I do it perfectly? Nope, not even… sure wish I could say I did. But I learned the hard way what you can learn from my mistakes. The times when I was gentle and really led by the Lord and served Danny well there was peace in my home. When I allowed my heart to get hard and bitterness to grow, tension rose, and we weren't united on much of anything. And that's no way to live at all.

Now I don't believe it's right for either party to be expected to take exclusive responsibility for the areas a marriage struggles usually. There are always two people involved, both are contributing, and each person must take personal responsibility for the role they play, even if it's simply being too compliant where blatant sin is present. We can't make someone else do anything, but we can choose to do the right thing no matter what anyone else chooses. We can choose to be the best version of self and entrust our spouse to God.

One thing the Lord often reminded me of, over our nearly 18 years of marriage, is that when we stand before Him, we will stand alone. We won't be able to say, "if it weren't for that man", "if it weren't for that woman", "those kids" etc. We will give an account based on our own personal responsibilities regardless of what anyone else did or didn't do. Because really when we're pointing at someone else there're three fingers pointing back at us. I may not have the power to change someone else, but I can certainly change the way I respond to them, how they impact me and how I love them.

When Danny and I first got married he didn't understand tithing, but I kept on and would pray about God dealing with him. Over the years he came to grab ahold of the Biblical principle especially after he saw time and again how the Lord would provide. He didn't need a lecture, he needed to see the tangible reality of that biblical principle being faithfully applied. Over time he wanted to make sure we were tithing. Glory to God!!

As godly women if we will obey the Lord and allow Him to transform us others will naturally be impacted. A wife & mother has a very strong influence in the family dynamics. As we stay yielded to the Lord, He will bring our marriages and families into order. We need not try to "fix" things or people but simply follow His lead and learn to love and serve them well.

People we are influencing learn far more by what they see us do, how they see us respond, and how we carry ourselves than what we say. If we are doers of the Word it will be well with them as they follow our lead.

Key Takeaways

- If we surrender to God's will for us individually, there's no need to fix anyone else.

- If we bring tithes & offerings to honor God, the devourer will be rebuked on our behalf, and we will live in abundance.

- God's way is always the best way.

Declarations:

❖ **According to Acts 16:31, as I believe in the Lord Jesus and allow Him to be my Lord and Savior, my household shall be saved. In Jesus name.**

("And they answered, Believe in the Lord Jesus Christ [give yourself up to Him, take yourself out of your own keeping and entrust yourself into His keeping] and you will be saved, [and this applies both to] you and your household as well.")

❖ **According to Matthew 6:33, as I seek first the kingdom of God and His righteousness ALL the things I have need of, shall be added unto me.**

("But seek ye first the kingdom of God, and his righteousness; and all these things shall be added unto you.")

Chapter 4

God's Way

"Be subject to one another out of reverence for Christ (the Messiah, the Anointed One). Wives, be subject (be submissive and adapt yourselves) to your own husbands as [a service] to the Lord. For the husband is head of the wife as Christ is the Head of the church, Himself the Savior of [His] body. As the church is subject to Christ, so let wives also be subject in everything to their husbands.

Husbands, love your wives, as Christ loved the church and gave Himself up for her, So that He might sanctify her, having cleansed her by the washing of water with the Word, That He might present the church to Himself in glorious splendor, without spot or wrinkle or any such things [that she might be holy and faultless]. Even so, husbands should love their wives as [being in a sense] their own bodies. He who loves his own wife loves himself. For no man ever hated his own flesh, but nourishes and carefully protects and cherishes it, as Christ does the church, because we are members (parts) of His body.

For this reason a man shall leave his father and his mother and shall be joined to his wife, and the two shall become one flesh. This mystery is very great, but I speak concerning [the relation of] Christ and the church. However, let each man of you [without exception] love his wife as [being in a sense] his very own self; and let the wife *see that she respects and reverences her husband [that she notices him, regards him, honors him, prefers him, venerates, and esteems him; and that she defers to him, praises him, and loves and admires him exceedingly]." Ephesians 5:21-33*

It's interesting how many people have chosen to sling these scriptures at their spouse to show how they're not measuring up. But God wants us to evaluate how we're personally doing, make any needed changes and trust Him to work on our spouse where needed. If both partners would focus on doing what they're supposed to do, instead of evaluating and criticizing where their spouse needs work, then both would end up being fulfilled. They would be preferring one another over themselves, which is what we're admonished to do in 1Corinthinas 13:4-7. And where we began this chapter in Ephesians 5:21, *"Be subject to one another out of reverence for Christ"*, cannot be left out nor ignored. How different would marriage look if both parties submitted themselves to God first and then to each other?

How different would the church look if we truly preferred one another and looked out for others instead of grasping at the survival mentality of self-preservation? Jesus tells us in Matthew 10:39 the key to true fulfillment, *"He that findeth his life shall lose it: and he that loseth his life for my sake shall find it."* That sounds so strange in contrast to what we've been taught and how society seems to work. But God has a better plan. The kingdom of heaven opposes the kingdom of the earth. It's completely opposite of the world's system. A gentle word turns away wrath. Give if you have a need. Bless those that curse you. If someone steals from you, give them more. And on and on.

We must decide, within ourselves, which kingdom we want to be a part of and benefit from. If we're Christians, then we belong to the Kingdom of Heaven but we have to choose to live and walk according to the standards and benefits of that kingdom. God says He's our vindicator, He is the righteous judge. Will we dare to trust Him with our marriages, our finances, our children?

One quote that often comes back to me is by Heidi Baker. She's a sold-out lover of Jesus and a momma to a great number of orphans. She often says, "lower, lower still". If we truly want to follow our Savior, we must decrease in our estimation. Now I'm not talking about the false humility that some want to put on. I'm talking about pushing aside our own interests and right to be heard and taking those things to God instead and trusting Him to bring forth all we have need of.

NOW WAIT!!

Don't throw this book down in frustration and walk away. I'm in no way implying that you must live some impoverished, unloved, pitiful existence. Quite the opposite. What I'm merely suggesting is not leaning on the arm of the flesh anymore to get things done. God said in Zechariah 4:6, *"it's not by might, nor by power but by My Spirit says the Lord"*. Over the last several years I've come to see that when I've attempted to get things done by my will, skill and tenacity things don't come out quite right. But when I lean not unto my own understanding and in all my ways I acknowledge Him, He makes my path straight.

His ways are higher than ours and He has a vantage point we don't have. He knows the end from the beginning. So why are we so quick to try to handle things ourselves and fail to consult with the One who has perfect insight into all? Sometimes we act like He doesn't even have our best interest at heart but that couldn't be further from the truth.

God loves His kids so very much and He wants to see us blessed beyond measure. Ponder this for a moment, what's a better testimony of a good parent? When their child is dirty, malnourished and love starved or when they're clean, well fed, well dressed, and full of life & joy? The latter of course. So why in the world would God not want you blessed if He wants ALL mankind to be saved and be in right relationship with Him?

Perhaps you haven't had good parents or life has been really hard and you're struggling to believe God is a good Father, like I was. (Not that I had bad parents, but I did have a difficult childhood and I've experienced many tragedies, obstacles and hardships in my life.) He already knows how you feel. He knows your thoughts, your heart's desires, and deepest hurts. King David was a man after God's own heart, why? I believe it's because he was real with God. He made mistakes, even some really big ones but He was quick to run to God and be transparent with Him.

The Lord's not afraid of your true feelings, in fact He wants to set you free and help you deal with the root of those feelings. So, if you're struggling to see Him as a good Father just take a moment and talk to Him. Ask Him to reveal to you any wrong mindsets you might have and to reveal Himself to you for who He truly is. He loves you so very much and He longs to be known by you.

Proper Alignment Brings Forth Blessing

We're gonna dive deep into some fairly controversial things here but please, prayerfully bear with me. If you've made it this far then you no doubt want all God has in His heart to give you. And if that's truly your desire then you must have a clear understanding of His will and His way of doing things.

With that said, even in a marriage that's not equally yoked it's very important that as wives we submit to our husbands, but not in the way the world has sold submission. We are to honor, respect, and defer to them. Eve was taken from Adams' side to walk beside him not from his foot to be walked on. Marriage is a partnership, and the man does have a greater responsibility before God for our families, but we are not called to be door mats. The two become ONE. One flesh. That means both contribute, both are vital, and both bring strengths to the table that the family needs. To be equally yoked don't we have to actually walk side-by-side?

I couldn't tell you how many times over the years I'd asked the Lord to "deal with that man", only to hear, "how about you?". The Lord was always more concerned about my character, my heart posture and my attitude than bringing some quick correction to him.

Time and again I've had to release my right to be angry or hold a grudge, to get and/or keep my heart right. I wish I could say I always did a great job of that but that'd be a lie. The lessons I'm sharing in this book, I've learned over the last 20 years but I'm sharing them in hopes of giving you "cheat codes" so that you can be years ahead of the game and not waste precious time and energy. You can learn to really fight well for your marriage, family, and future and see the hand of God do what the hand of man never could.

If there's anything the last few years have taught me it's that time goes by so very quickly, and life is but a vapor. It's much wiser to spend time on the things that really matter and pick our battles. Not every battle that presents itself deserves your attention. The ones that really matter are won far more effectively on our knees before the King than with us fretting and fighting to get our own way. He's exponentially better at securing victories than we are, and we can trust Him even with our most precious relationships. We can fully trust Him with the deepest part of our hearts even if man has failed us time and again.

Our faithfulness to do what the Lord instructs is not wasted, even if our spouse seems very lost. In 1 Corinthians 7:14 it says, *"For*

the unbelieving husband is sanctified [that is, he receives the blessings granted] through his [Christian] wife, and the unbelieving wife is sanctified through her believing husband. Otherwise, your children would be [ceremonially] unclean, but as it is they are holy".
So don't grow weary, friend. Stay faithful, stay in the Word and fight on your knees for your marriage and family. God sees you and He hears your hearts cry. Your prayers have not fallen on deaf ears. He is moving things around on your behalf and you will see the mighty hand of God if you faint not.

A Word fitly spoken

Sometimes the greatest strategy in winning a battle is the ability to hold your peace and not say anything. Now I'm not talking about the silent treatment, this technique is FAR more advantageous and healthier than that. I couldn't tell you how many times over the years I would get so frustrated because I'd tried to tell my late husband something and he just wouldn't listen. But someone else would come along and say the very same thing and it was like the Gospel truth to him. I started to realize that if I really needed him to get something or see something, especially in light of scripture, I needed to go over his head.

The Holy Spirit can speak to those we love far better than we can, especially about deep-rooted issues. In the beginning he didn't understand tithing but as I stayed strong on scripture, walked in obedience, and continued to pray the Lord opened his eyes over time and he started to see that it was God's hand on our finances that was enabling us to even survive.

There were certain times when, looking back, I wish I would've held my tongue more. I don't recall where I first heard this analogy, but it's stuck with me all these years. Try taking a feather pillow up to the top of a mountain, ripping it open while a big gust of wind blows through and carries the feathers far & wide, then try to regather all the feathers. That would be an impossible feat. So, it is with our words. It's a far better practice to hold our tongue because once words are spoken, we can never take them back. Proverbs 14:27 says, *"He that hath knowledge spareth his words: and a man of understanding is of an excellent spirit"*.

I've prayed for many years that the Lord would put a guard on my mouth and help me to bridle my tongue. One little trick I've found is that if I really feel like giving someone a piece of my mind, then I'm likely not being governed by the mind of Christ, that's just my flesh talking. I need to prayerfully wait, check my heart with the Lord and receive any necessary correction BEFORE I speak. It would be nice if we could just arrive at this level of control, but it requires intentionally staying sensitive to the Lord's leading and not pursuing our own will and right to be heard.

Another lesson on the tongue is being careful to only speak life. In difficult relationships it can be easy to focus on the negative and highlight what's wrong, but we should water what we desire to see grow. Proverbs 18:21 says, *"Death and life are in the power of the tongue: and they that love it shall eat the fruit thereof"*. Amen or ouch!! As I said earlier, the reality we find ourselves living in is greatly determined by the words we speak. If we aren't careful, we can fence ourselves in by our words.

Proverbs 21:9 says, *"It is better to dwell in a corner of the housetop, than with a brawling woman in a wide house."* We don't want our husbands to cringe at the thought of coming home or preferring to hang out on the rooftop to being with us. We're called to be peacemakers and a helpmeet for them. Often this will require us not speaking what's on our mind. Especially if they can't receive what we're saying, for whatever reason. Taking those things to God is a far better alternative.

We can speak our marriage and family right into sure victory too. You see life AND death are in the power of the tongue, so we get to choose. Deuteronomy 30:19 says, *"I call heaven and earth to record this day against you, that I have set before you life and death, blessing and cursing: therefore choose life, that both thou and thy seed may live."* As we see in this passage, our choices not only affect us but our families for generations to come. And even if there is a long list of failed marriages, brokenness and difficult relationships in your family tree, that can all stop with you. You can choose to do the hard work of doing life God's way and setting up the generations to come for marital bliss and relational harmony. Doesn't that sound like something worthy of temporary sacrifice?

Key Takeaways

- *"A soft answer turns away wrath, but grievous words stir up anger". Proverbs 15:1*

- We must watch our words because we are creating.

- Our influence will be great as we allow the Lord to have His way in our lives.

Declarations:

❖ According to Proverbs 18:21, I choose to speak life and eat the good fruit of my words, I refuse to speak death.

("*Death and life are in the power of the tongue: and they that love it shall eat the fruit thereof".)*

❖ Father, I thank You that according to 1 Corinthians 7:14, because I am a Christian, my spouse is sanctified, and my children are holy.

(*"For the unbelieving husband is sanctified [that is, he receives the blessings granted] through his [Christian] wife, and the unbelieving wife is sanctified through her believing husband. Otherwise, your children would be [ceremonially] unclean, but as it is they are holy".)*

Chapter 5

Talk to HIM

"Do not fret or have any anxiety about anything, but in every circumstance and in everything, by prayer and petition (definite requests), with thanksgiving, continue to make your wants known to God." Philippians 4:6

Far too many people approach God from their intellect, but He is Spirit, and we must "worship Him in Spirit & in Truth." (John 4:24) A relationship with God cannot be fostered merely in the mind and through studiously reading the black and white pages of the Bible. Some people will miss heaven and the wonderful intimacy of real relationship with Him by the distance between their head to their heart. They have a knowledge of God but never give Him access to their heart and truly connect with Him through their spirit. I've seen intellectuals who know the Word in their minds but have a very difficult time grabbing it with their hearts. They read the Bible like any other book but don't meet the Author there and don't allow The Word to read them.

One good way to bypass the brain is to start worshiping Him with your whole heart and soul. To really pour your love out onto God through thanksgiving and praise. Set your affections on Him and talk to Him all throughout the day. And then… listen. If you and your best friend were riding in a car and one of you was doing all the talking that wouldn't make for a very good relationship. So why do we so often do that with God? It can be easy only to talk to Him when things are going bad or when something crazy good happens. But there's a whole lot of life that happens in between those two extremes and He's the God of the in-between times too. He wants to hear from His kids and dialog back and forth with us.

John 10:27 says, *"The sheep that are My own hear My voice and listen to Me; I know them, and they follow Me"*. It's astonishing to me how many believers don't believe that God talks to them, "unbelieving believers" if you will. They wrestle with knowing they've heard from Him. Occasionally we all probably wrestle with this but this ought not be how it usually is. If this is your reality, there's no condemnation but it's time for you to hear Him and to know when you have. You can start by declaring that verse over yourself. "God, Your Word says your sheep hear your voice and they follow You. I know I'm one of your sheep and I know that You are teaching me to hear You and I will not follow the voice of another. Thank You Lord for fine tuning my ears to hear and obey you. In Jesus name." He's not upset when we ask for what we lack and it's His desire that we would be confident in our ability to hear Him. In fact, at times our very life could depend on it.

I'm reminded of a time when the Lord told me to "slow down and look" as I approached a green light. Just then, a car blazed through their red light. Or the time when the Lord told me to go all the way into my baby girl's room when I was just ready to go to bed after a long day. As I went in, at His warning, I found she was being strangled by her untucked crib sheet. God saved her life that night. Glory to His name!! There've been other times that He's spoken to me about where something was that I was looking for or given me wisdom and insight far beyond my own. His voice brings life to us. WE MUST HEAR & OBEY HIM! Especially in the days ahead. Our lives and the lives of those around us could depend on it.

One of the ways I began stewarding the voice of God was sitting at my kitchen table with my Bible, journal, and a pen. I would invite the Holy Spirit to teach me and give me revelation about the Word and then we'd talk through the scripture, and I'd write what I felt He was revealing. As I look back over the many journals I've accumulated, they are priceless treasures that I cherish dearly. Inside each one He's given me instruction, direction, encouragement, and wisdom that I desperately needed and that I draw from to this day. As we're faithful to steward the little ways He speaks to us He will reveal more. The Word says if we're faithful with the little we'll be entrusted with much and I've found this to be very true. He's faithful to His Word. He even watches over His Word to perform it according to Jeremiah 1:12.

He also talks through songs, other people, nature and on and on. He's not limited like we are. He knows everything about everything so He can speak in multi-faceted ways. The question is not whether He's speaking but, are we listening and perceiving what He's saying?

When you sit down and decide to make your time with the Lord a priority or steward His voice better, don't be surprised if distractions come. There's a very real enemy of your soul that knows how important it is for you to get into the Word and to hear God's voice. Often, he will send distractions to try to derail your God ordained path and destiny and sometimes it's our own flesh that will rear up and bring distraction. But I encourage you to press in with determination in your heart and don't give up. The lover of your soul is well worth any struggle or sacrifice.

One trick that I often use when diving into the Word and trying to get my mind quiet is to keep some paper or a notebook handy to jot down all the thoughts that try to invade my time with Him. You know, the list of to-dos, the grocery list, the people we need to call, etc. I've found that if I write those things down when they come up, they will stay safely parked on that paper until I'm ready to tackle them. Then I can focus my attention on the only One worthy.

The Secret Place of True Rest

Now let's look further into that passage… *"And God's peace [shall be yours, that tranquil state of a soul assured of its salvation through Christ, and so fearing nothing from God and being content with its earthly lot of whatever sort that is, that peace] which transcends all understanding shall garrison and mount guard over your hearts and minds in Christ Jesus. ",* Philippians 4:7. Personally, I often see my time with the Lord as climbing up on my Daddy's lap, especially when I'm broken and hurting. It's always a place of true peace and rest, especially when in the natural it seems logical to freak out. When we really bring our concerns, thoughts and even ourselves to the Lord, He takes those things and gives us Himself. Wow!!! The heavenly exchange!

Perfect love casts out fear. (1John 4:18) And God is perfect love. (1John 4:8) We can find sweet assurance, peace, and unconditional love in the presence of The King. He already knows every detail, every thought, even the bad ones, and He loves us anyway. Some want to run away from God when they mess up, I know I did. But what we really need to do is run TO Him and allow Him to change us.

Our passage goes on to admonish us as to what we should be focusing on, what we should replace those cares, fears, concerns, and worries with as we lay them before the King. *"For the rest, brethren, whatever is true, whatever is worthy of reverence and is honorable and seemly, whatever is just, whatever is pure, whatever is lovely and lovable, whatever is kind and winsome and gracious, if there is any virtue and excellence, if there is anything worthy of praise, think on and weigh and take account of these things [fix your minds on them]."* Philippians 4:7-8

The truth of the matter is, God doesn't want us weighed down with the cares of this world. He wants us completely free and where the Spirit of the Lord is there's freedom. (2 Corinthians 3:17) Just like the key passage for this chapter says, we are to be anxious for nothing but to take all things to God. He even cares about the minute details of your life. When we're in relationship with Him it can be like other close relationships in many ways. For instance, if you can't find your keys, you could ask someone else in your house and they'd likely help you find them. So why not ask God? He knows exactly where they are. Why not practice, daily, having an open dialog with the Lord?

My Closest Friend

I couldn't begin to tell you how many times I've felt all alone only to discover the Lord was right there with me. When I turn my attention towards Him, I always find that He's right there and He has been all along. So often people reason that they don't want to bother God, or He has much more important things to do than spend time with them but that couldn't be further from the truth. Fact of the matter is, God is MUCH BIGGER and far more interested in relationship with us than most understand. He's omni-present, that means He's everywhere, at all times. In the Word we see that He's an "ever present help in time of need". (Psalm 46:1) Ever present not just sometimes or occasionally.

John 15:4-8 takes it much further…,"*Abide in Me, and I in you. As the branch cannot bear fruit of itself, unless it abides in the vine, neither can you, unless you abide in Me. I am the vine; you are the branches. He who abides in Me, and I in him, bears much fruit; for without Me you can do nothing. If anyone does not abide in Me, he is cast out as a branch and is withered; and they gather them and throw them into the fire, and they are burned. If you abide in Me, and My words abide in you, you will ask what you desire, and it shall be done for you. By this My Father is glorified, that you bear much fruit; so you will be My disciples.*" The enemy does not want us to have a real relationship with God because that's what's required for true salvation, liberation, and fulfillment. We must abide in Him and Him in us.

This takes me to a journal entry the Lord brought me back to this morning: *"So much of humanity is bustling by, rarely giving pause to My presence. Many who know I exist scarcely acknowledge My nearness. I long for My creation, My beloved ones to turn towards Me and tune into My voice. To seek Me first so that I can order their steps. I want to guide each one and keep them from stumbling. To lavish My love on them and unveil their true identities. But few will listen. Few joyfully receive My correction and Fatherly love. Few will turn to me when it's not an hour of need. Yet they don't realize that they, always, are in need. They must be connected to Me to even fulfill their destiny. I am the vine, you are the branches. Apart from Me there's no life, no fullness, no lasting abundance. But in Me is fullness of Joy, Life & Love."*

Can you hear the heart of the Father? He longs to connect with you. Not to merely be a 911 God but our closest friend, confidant, and Savior. The moments of sweet intimacy with the King prepare us for everything else. In His presence is fullness of joy, peace, rest, and the purest love that has ever existed. That longing every human being has deep in their soul really is a God shaped hole. Many try to fill it with sex, drugs, money, achievement, friends, busyness and on and on but to no avail. Only God can fill the deepest longings of the human soul. Only God.

Do you realize that God knew every single mistake, every bad attitude, every imperfection you would ever have or make, and He said…. *"I want that one! I made them for myself. I long to lavish My love on them and unveil their created purpose. Yep, that one!! Flaws and all. If they'll just come to Me, I will give them rest. I will heal their wounds and wash them clean. I will give them beauty for ashes and joy for mourning. If they'd only turn their gaze My way and let Me really come in, be Lord & Savior, and walk hand in hand with Me the rest of their days. Oh, what adventures we could have."*

He loves you!!! I can feel His presence as I pen this. I can feel the longing of His heart for you. His desire to have access and heal the most intimate and broken places of your heart and home. No matter what you've heard…. He died for YOU!! And He longs to have your whole heart. He can be fully trusted with it. Unlike any mere mortal, He'll never betray you, walk away from you or abandon you.

We are the ones who choose. We choose how much of Him we come to know and how much access He has in our lives. He won't force Himself on us. He has no desire to command someone to love Him, it doesn't work like that. He desires genuine love just as we do.

How loved would you feel if you knew someone was only "loving you" out of obligation? If someone's heart isn't in it, it shows. That kind of relationship always leaves us feeling empty, rejected, and unloved. All throughout scripture we see how God desires what is pure and holy. He is the God of authenticity. No false weights and balances, no fake worship, no eloquent ramblings and certainly no fake and shallow love is welcome with Him. Only what's genuine. And boy is He ever worth genuinely laying your life down for! He's the only One I've found truly worthy.

Oh, how I treasure His touch, His voice, His presence. If you haven't felt that or you're longing for more, take a moment and ask Him. We have not because we ask not. I've made it a regular practice to stir myself up and press in and cry out for more of Him. I'm not content!! It's kind of like eating your favorite meal.... Often, we keep eating after we're full because it's just that good. Well, He's WAY better than that!! The Word says, "taste and see" and that those who hunger and thirst for righteousness shall be filled. (Righteousness is right standing with God) Come to Him genuinely desirous of more of Him and see if He'll not answer.

I dare you!

Key Takeaways

- It is God's will to not only talk to us but to have a daily relationship with us, with mutual dialog.

- Always run TO Him never from Him, especially if you mess up.

- Journal what the Lord is saying and compare what you're hearing to the Word. He'll never contradict His Word.

Declarations:

❖ According to John 10:27, I hear the voice of God, I listen to Him, and I follow Him because I am His sheep.

("The sheep that are My own hear My voice and listen to Me; I know them, and they follow Me")

❖ According to Matthew 11:28, anytime life gets too hard I can come to God, and He gives me rest.

("Come unto me, all ye that labor and are heavy laden, and I will give you rest.")

Chapter 6

Praise is a Weapon

"O Lord, thou art my God; I will exalt thee, I will praise thy name; for thou hast done wonderful things; thy counsels of old are faithfulness and truth." Isaiah 25:1

"The LORD is my strength and my shield; my heart trusted in him, and I am helped: therefore, my heart greatly rejoiceth; and with my song will I praise him." Psalm 28:7

"Why art thou cast down, O my soul? and why art thou disquieted within me? Hope thou in God: for I shall yet praise him, who is the health of my countenance, and my God." Psalm 42:11

Being a believer does not mean life is all smooth sailing and we never face challenges. Sometimes life can seem like it's raging all around us. We can feel like a ship lost at sea being tossed about by the unrelenting waves. Those are the moments we must remember to fix our gaze on Jesus. Just as Peter did when he walked on the water. We may not feel like reading the Word, talking to the Lord or being obedient. It may not even feel like we can see the hand of God in our situation, but feelings often can't be trusted. The fastest way to shift the atmosphere and force our flesh into submission and get back into right alignment with God is to crank up some anointed praise music and dance and sing until everything shifts.

Have a praise break!

Perhaps this chapter found you having a moment like that. Wanting to press in deep down but feeling overwhelmed and lethargic. Shake it off!!! Rise up, turn on your favorite praise song and fix your gaze on the King. Very soon you'll find that not only has your attitude shifted but your situation begins to look different too. Why not take a moment right now and shift that atmosphere?

Go ahead.... I'll wait.

There's something so powerful about overlooking our circumstances and fixing our gaze on The King! He's so worthy of our undying affections. He's beyond worthy of our most lavish praise!

When we come to God with a sacrifice of praise, He shows up. Psalm 51:17 says, *"The sacrifices of God are a broken spirit: a broken and a contrite heart, O God, thou wilt not despise."* He's near to the broken and contrite. He weeps and rejoices with us. Have you ever been around someone you love who was hurting but when you tried to console them, they pushed you away? That's how we respond to God sometimes when all He wants to do is comfort, heal and restore us.

If we're in a tough relationship where we feel rejected, unloved, and taken for granted it can be tough to allow the ones who really do love us, unconditionally, to have access to our vulnerable places. This is one area that the Lord has worked with me for years. And if I'm being candid, I still occasionally have to be reminded that some people really do genuinely love me simply because of who I am as a person. Not for what I can do for them, what I'm called to or any perceived benefit our relationship might provide.

Do you know that God loves you unconditionally? Your works or lack of work doesn't make Him love you more nor less. Walking through life with Him and taking His will and emotions into account makes Him feel loved just as it does for us in our earthly relationships. When we choose to really spend time with someone it sends a message of friendship, kindness, and love.

Often, people don't know how to express or share the love they have for us. They can be hesitant because of past hurts and insecurities. But God isn't that way. He knows exactly how to give and receive love and longs to teach us what true and healthy love looks like. He loves to spend time with us, and we can have the best talks and adventures with the Lord. God is inviting us into a very intimate and personal relationship with Him. One that fulfills the deepest longings and desires of our souls.

He's not a far-off God. That's who I thought He was until I really encountered Him in February of '02. He's a loving Father who longs to be close to us. To walk and talk with us. And guess what, He not only enjoys us praising and singing to Him, but He reciprocates. Zephaniah 3:17 says, *"The Lord your God is in the midst of you, a Mighty One, a Savior [Who saves]! He will rejoice over you with joy; He will rest [in silent satisfaction] and in His love He will be silent and make no mention [of past sins, or even recall them]; He will exult over you with singing."*

Can you believe that? The uncreated One, the God of all creation sings over YOU! Now please don't mishear me. I'm not in any way saying God worships us, only He is worthy of worship, but He adores us, He sings over us, and we are the apple of His eye according to Psalm 17. He hand-fashioned each one of us, exactly as

He intended in our mother's womb and our births brought Him great joy. (See Jeremiah 1:5)

Daddy's Lap

Perhaps you find yourself in a loveless or a little love marriage and you're lonely and longing to share your heart and have true intimacy with your spouse. No matter the temptation, don't run to the arms or affections of another person. Don't allow yourself to get close to a co-worker or caught up in online conversation, even on Facebook, with someone of the opposite sex, or anything in between for that matter. These things only cause us to develop feelings for someone other than our spouse and they open the door to the devil, whose only mission is to steal, kill and destroy you, your marriage & family and to drag you to hell.

Personally, one of my love languages is deep, heartfelt conversation. So, while the obvious good looks and blatant sexual temptation didn't allure me, it was the intellectually stimulating conversation with the opposite sex that I really had to guard myself against. When you're feeling lonely or rejected, it can feel really nice to have the attention of another, especially an attractive and intelligent member of the opposite sex. But God takes the marriage covenant very seriously and so should we. 2 Corinthians 10:5 says, *"Casting down imaginations, and every high thing that exalteth itself against the knowledge of God, and bringing into captivity every thought to the obedience of Christ"*. Every thought that comes your way is not necessarily your thought and you can refuse to receive it. Bring those thoughts that are contrary to The Word under Christ' authority and do not entertain them.

Jesus told us that even looking at someone with lust in our eyes is the same as committing adultery with them. Now that may sound like a strong stance but read it for yourself, *"Ye have heard that it was said by them of old time, thou shalt not commit adultery: But I say unto you, that whosoever looketh on a woman to lust after her hath committed adultery with her already in his heart."*, Matthew 5:27-28. While the scripture says her, we can obviously infer that He meant male or female. God looks at the heart and we must make sure we keep clean hands and a pure heart.

Now, we ALWAYS need to guard our eye and ear gates but even more if we're in a difficult marriage or relationship. Proverbs 4:23 says, *"Keep thy heart with all diligence; for out of it are the issues of life",* KJV. But the NLT says, *"Guard your heart above all else, for it determines the course of your life".* To guard, according to Miriam Webster is a defensive position (as in boxing); the act or duty of protecting or defending; to protect from danger especially by watchful attention: make secure; to tend to carefully: preserve, and protect, just to name a few.

Far too many people go about life vulnerable to the attacks of the enemy and don't employ the Word of God, but you are much wiser than that. And if you haven't been up to this point, no condemnation, but I pray you are growing in wisdom as you read this, in Jesus' name. If the Bible says we need to guard our hearts, we'd better take heed of it. Our Father doesn't just say things for the sake of saying them, any more than we as parents usually do. He wants to protect, guide, and direct our steps. He cares more for us than we care for ourselves.

And I must admonish you, from personal experience, the importance of guarding your heart and not giving a single opportunity for temptation, especially if you're fighting for your marriage. Instead, get alone with the Father, climb up on His lap and allow Him to meet your needs. There have been many times over the years that

I've done this and literally felt the Lord wrap His arms around me as I cried. He really is an ever-present help in time of need and He's near to us, especially in our brokenness.

I couldn't tell you how many times I've tucked away with the Lord, my Bible, journal, and a cup of coffee and allowed Him to console and counsel my soul. I've cried out to Him, and He answers. Like I said earlier, He really does want to have conversations with us and to care for our hearts and emotions. He wants to teach us how to navigate through the challenging times and He wants to celebrate the wins with us.

Even if every single person has failed you, God never will. He's the gentlest, most loving, most intimate, and personal being I've ever encountered. I've never tasted a love more pure, sincere, selfless, or fulfilling. All of my life I'd longed for someone who would love me completely, unconditionally and endlessly and while I've rarely seen that in another person, God Almighty always fits the bill. So, if there's a longing for true love in the depths of your being, look no further, the King is the answer.

"Beloved, let us love one another, for love is (springs) from God; and he who loves [his fellowmen] is begotten (born) of God and

is coming [progressively] to know and understand God [to perceive and recognize and get a better and clearer knowledge of Him]. He who does not love has not become acquainted with God [does not and never did know Him], for God is love.

In this the love of God was made manifest (displayed) where we are concerned: in that God sent His Son, the only begotten or unique [Son], into the world so that we might live through Him. In this is love: not that we loved God, but that He loved us and sent His Son to be the propitiation (the atoning sacrifice) for our sins. Beloved, if God loved us so [very much], we also ought to love one another. No man has at any time [yet] seen God. But if we love one another, God abides (lives and remains) in us and His love (that love which is essentially His) is brought to completion (to its full maturity, runs its full course, is perfected) in us!" John 4:7-12

It's truly from our love relationship with God that we come to fully love each other. God is love. It's His character, His nature and as we become more and more like our Father, we will have a greater capacity to love.

If you're married but you wake up not "feeling" married, are you any less married? Of course not! If you love God but don't "feel" like praising or reading the Word, or spending time with Him are you any less His? No! But you must press past how you "feel" and love Him well anyway. As you do, you'll soon find yourself swept up in His glorious presence. And you will notice your cares have fallen away, the heaviness is gone, and you'll find your song, dance, and lasting joy in the presence of The King.

Key Takeaways

- Let love abound in and through you.

- Praise for your breakthrough.

- Guard your heart!

Declarations:

❖ According to Proverbs 4:23, I choose to guard my heart with all diligence, so the course of my life is good.

"Guard your heart above all else, for it determines the course of your life".

❖ I will protect my heart, my marriage, and my family from the works of the enemy. I will love my family well and I will walk according to the love of God and not be led by my feelings. In Jesus mighty name!

Chapter 7

Healthy Boundaries

When Danny & I first got married there was a real imbalance in relationships with the opposite sex, especially where my late husband was concerned. Within the first week of marriage, we'd agreed that any friends of the opposite sex that weren't interested in spending time with both of us were obviously in it for the wrong reasons and they'd have to go. That being said, any friends of the opposite sex should not be trying to communicate with us privately. The Bible admonishes us to be wise as serpents yet gentle as doves in Matthew 10:16.

As we set out to really build God centered, kingdom marriages and families we must not think for a moment that the enemy won't try to send division and discord. For a marriage to be strong and stand through the storms of life we must set boundaries to safeguard and protect our covenantal unions.

I recall when we were getting married a "female friend" of his expected a personal invitation from him and refused to come to our wedding because she simply got invited like everyone else did. That was a HUGE red flag!! That's not how a person acts who's supportive of your marriage. Danny had to sever that relationship for our marriage's sake. She tried at different times, over the years, to get him to come to her house alone but NEVER showed any interest in even meeting me, the woman he'd chosen to spend his life with. Hence the quotes on "female friend". That's not the behavior of a true friend at all. True friends will want to develop a healthy relationship with your spouse as well because they literally become your other half according to scripture and they should be the most important person in your life.

If you'd be uncomfortable handing your spouse your unlocked phone you might want to prayerfully consider why. There should be no secrets from them except perhaps an occasional surprise party or present that they'll soon be privy to, otherwise we should be an open book to our spouses. Not everyone is desirous of that sort of relationship, but I question their reasoning. Eve was created from the rib of Adam; not sure you can get any closer than that. Genesis 2:24-25 shows us God's plan for marriage, *"Therefore shall a man leave his father and his mother and shall cleave unto his wife, and they shall be one flesh. And they were both naked, the man and his wife, and were not ashamed."*

Can you leave any part of your body behind when you go somewhere? If the two become one-flesh then there should be nothing they don't share with each other, except maybe bodily functions. LOL! I for one could completely do without sharing bathroom times and all unnecessary sharing in that realm. Each to their own but I'm personally more private in that area.

However, secrecy in marriage is an area where far too many couples have gone wrong. Way too many live, as we did, separate lives yet co-existing in the same house. Having separate friend groups, interests, hobbies and rarely doing anything together besides family dinner and an occasional date night or weekend getaway. Not that you should never do anything without your spouse. It's important to have guy or girl time with your friends. But your friends should interact with your spouse in a healthy way and neither spouse should be a completely different person around their friends in their spouse's absence.

Marriage isn't supposed to be merely co-existing. If it is, then what's the point of getting married or being in a serious relationship at all? When we say "I do" we should be saying yes to building a life together, raising a family together and growing old together, not merely existing and tolerating one another.

Recently I was at a prayer meeting at church and the Lord started talking to me about marriage. He told me He's raising up Kingdom Couples that will, *"honor the covenant they made before Me. I am re-establishing the marriage bed. It will be deemed pure and holy again, an act of worship unto Me.*

Wrong mindsets, generational curses and cultural norms have polluted marriage, even among My people. This ought not be. I am raising up fiery Kingdom Couples who will be used strategically to restore My plans for marriage. My family shall be established in righteousness, holiness and purity."

God's plan for marriage has never changed. Genesis 1:27-28 tells us His plan, *"So God created man in his own image, in the image of God created he him; male and female created he them. And God blessed them, and God said unto them, be fruitful, and multiply, and replenish the earth, and subdue it: and have dominion over the fish of the sea, and over the fowl of the air, and over every living thing that moveth upon the earth."* Marriage was instituted for multiplication and walking in united authority and taking dominion as Christ's ambassadors.

It's so sad that I should even have to address this, but the fact of the matter is, according to scripture and according to God Almighty, the uncreated One, marriage is to be between one natural born MAN and one natural born WOMAN. No other combination is honorable or holy and no other union will be protected or blessed by God, NONE. No other union can even sustain life through reproduction, hence further proof of God's original plan. It matters not the opinion of man. Hebrews 13:8 reaffirms to us, *"Jesus Christ the same yesterday, and today, and forever"*. He is God and He changes NOT. I could go way deeper into this topic and what the scripture says but that is not the intended focus of this book. If you are wrestling with what I just said I encourage you to look at the scriptures yourself and discover the truth in God's Word and how He feels about the subject. The truth will set you free!!

It's time for godly men and women to rise up and stand for what our Father says is right and stop settling for anything less. We must not look so much like the world that they can't even tell who our Father is. In fact, if we look too much like the world, we should personally evaluate who our Father actually is because a true son or daughter should look like their Daddy. The problem is there's been far too much compromise in the body of Christ and the percentage of compromise and divorce in the church doesn't look much different than the world. That's really not ok! The world should be able to see stark differences in how we live and who we are if we're truly following Jesus.

If we want a marriage that will stand the test of time, we must allow God to be at the center and work with Him to see His plan fulfilled in our marriages and families. We must not merely set "healthy boundaries", but we need to make sure they're Biblically sound ones as well. Furthermore, a couple cohabiting is not under the blessing either. We cannot live in what God calls sin and expect Him to bless it. He has not changed, and He never will so we are the ones that need to change to fit what our Holy God says is right.

If you're currently in a situation like that, repent and make it right by either marrying or moving out. God doesn't want you living in willful sin and separated from Him. Isaiah 59:2 shows us, *"...your iniquities have separated between you and your God, and your sins have hid his face from you, that he will not hear"*. Romans 6:23

says, *"For the wages of sin is death; but the gift of God is eternal life through Jesus Christ our Lord".* He wants us to live eternally with Him, but we cannot live in willful sin and still enter heaven. 1John 1:9 says, *"If we confess our sins, he is faithful and just to forgive us our sins, and to cleanse us from all unrighteousness".* He's provided a way out if we'll take it.

Some are no doubt sitting here thinking, get on with it lady I came to hear how to fight for my marriage not about sin. But if we don't take a solid stance against sin we will embrace it and end up in hell for eternity. Nothing on this side of heaven matters in light of that. My late husband danced dangerously close to the edge of hell. But all glory to God, he had a praying wife as well as other prayer warriors lifting him up and God made a masterful chess move the day he died. Not everyone's story ends with that sort of grace. Perhaps I'll get into that later, but you need to realize how very personal and real the truths are that I'm sharing with you.

It is paramount that we structure our marriages, homes, and families on the unshakable foundation of Jesus Christ. John 1:1 tells us, "In the beginning was the Word, the Word was with God and the Word was God Himself". That Bible you hold in your hands is Jesus on paper. He is the cornerstone we are to build upon. James 1:22 says, *"But be ye doers of the word, and not hearers only, deceiving your own selves"*. We will run amiss every single time if the Word is not in us and governing how we live. This flesh is desirous of sinful things, but we must buffet the flesh and bring it under the full authority of the Word of God.

What's Hidden Shall Be Revealed

"For there is nothing covered, that shall not be revealed; neither hid, that shall not be known." Luke 12:2

As I said earlier, we need to be transparent where our spouse is concerned. I'm going to share some things in this chapter that are very personal, but I believe this story must be told. Unfortunately, some of the details are far too common in many households these days. Funny thing is, years ago the Lord told Danny & I that our marriage would be used to minister to other couples, little did we know, it would actually be in his death that this word would come to pass.

When he and I got married, unknown to me, he was an alcoholic and secretly addicted to painkillers. I knew when we were friends that he'd smoked pot but had quit, or so he said. I do believe he wanted to quit, that he wanted to do right by our family and become the man God made him to be, he just didn't know how. There were a few different godly men that reached out to him over the years, but the fact of the matter is we all have free will and we must personally choose. No one else can choose for us.

Instead of coming to me in transparency, humility, and honesty, so we could walk through his struggles together, he hid, and he lied. There were different times when he'd quit. He even went to rehab twice and seemed to be making great strides towards freedom and our marriage seemed to be well on its way to being healed and full of love. But unless we allow the light to fully shine in the dark places, revealing anything lurking there, allowing God to really set us free and do the work to stay free, we live in bondage and the enemy gets to beat us up. Not because that's what God has for us, but we can't serve two masters. We are the ones who choose.

There're a lot of counseling methods out there and believe me, we tried many, but the only one that really works and brings complete transformation, is JESUS. The anointed One & lover of our souls. He knows how to go into the deep places of the soul and get to the root of the issues and bring about healing that goes much deeper than the hand or words of man ever could.

My late husband struggled with love, receiving and giving. Because of the life he'd lived he buried things most of his life. You know, the hurts, pains, grief, disappointments, and rejections. When we bury things like that, they don't stay buried. And when they start to come up to be dealt with, many people will self-medicate, overindulge in food or sex, dive deep into work, go shopping, etc. Anything to ease the pain and not deal with the real issues. That's a very unhealthy and dangerous way to live.

As we lift those we love before the King and refuse to embrace offense, rejection, and bitterness the Lord Himself will work on our behalf. He'll show us what to say, when and how to say it and what not to do or say. We need the Lord to show us how to fight and what to pray. You see as the appointed head of the home the husband must be in agreement with God's will and establishing His plans for the family. If the man is not fully surrendered to God, it can leave the family vulnerable. Now I saw, many times over, how God protected our family in spite of the decisions he was making, and I know that's fruit from the verse I shared earlier about the believer sanctifying their spouse.

It's so important for both husband and wife to be united in the ways of God but if you aren't, don't become disheartened, we weren't united like God intended but the Lord moved anyway. Not to the measure He could've had we been united, but our family still saw the blessings, protection, and provision of the Lord. Don't grow weary friend. God isn't done with you or your marriage.

Personally, I'd told the Lord I'd white knuckle it and honor the covenant we'd made before Him no matter what it cost me. You know.... die to self and allow my needs and wants to go to sleep for the sake of staying and honoring what I'd committed to before God. Danny was not an abusive man with a bad heart. He simply didn't know how to love or how to stay free from the shackles of addiction and he would often draw back, away from me and our family. Much of our marriage I was very lonely and desperate for change but had to constantly turn to the Lord for help, direction, fulfillment, and peace. I'm in no way writing this book thinking I did everything right, there's plenty I'd change if I could go back. But we don't have that luxury, do we?

And if our story can help even one person, one couple, overcome and win in marriage, my transparency will be worthwhile. God called me to write this to give you keys for some doors you've been banging on. He didn't relent in provoking me to pen these words, because He wants YOU to be free and to walk in victory! May He grant you the wisdom and grace to boldly walk through, to miss the enemies' traps and fight well for your marriage & family. It'll be well worth it. And all of heaven will rejoice as you work with the Lord to truly build a Kingdom marriage.

We Must Heed the Warnings

Danny struggled with depression, addiction, unforgiveness and unprocessed grief and he didn't know how to get fully free and stay free from the snare of the enemy. Addictions are all too common and they're strong snares from the enemy that, sometimes, cost people their life. About a year and a half before he stepped into eternity, the Lord had me warn him that if he didn't change his ways, he'd have an untimely death. Unfortunately, he didn't heed the warning.

I fully believe in finding compromise in marriage and partnering with your spouse but when it comes to the Lord, keep running your race, even if they choose not to. Do not forfeit your relationship with the Lord for anything. Over the years my relationship with Jesus is what sustained me, it's helped me fight, to stay strong in the midst of life shaking battles. And to be quite honest... it's why I stayed when some would've left.

Over the years we both played our parts in not fostering a healthy marriage and home life. And while I am so grateful to have been afforded the luxury to be at home with our kids, I struggled with bitterness, loneliness, resentment and unforgiveness. And since I'd had a life, before our marriage, full of tragedy, sin, abuse, and instability, I took his addictions and lack of interest in me very personally. That made it very hard to accept love and to acknowledge I had worth and value. Even when he would try to extend love, I found it so hard to receive.

There was one point in our marriage where I'd grown so cold and so hard towards him that I literally couldn't even feel it when he touched me. I remember him touching my arm and I knew something was seriously wrong because I couldn't even feel it.

That was a wakeup call for me around 2011 that I was changing, I was becoming someone I didn't even like, and it was because I'd not guarded my heart. I'd allowed the hurts and disappointments to harden me to the point that I didn't even recognize myself. So, we separated. I even started justifying drinking a glass of wine each night to "unwind". What a lie from the pit of hell. Alcohol doesn't help you unwind, it just makes you numb to the reality and the consequences of sin.

That season brought me dangerously close to the edge of losing who I was and all I held dear to me. Giving into sin sounded more and more appealing as I wallowed in my pain. I'm so very thankful that the Lord protected me, and he even had Danny praying and fasting for our marriage in that season.

In my heart I was done. Done sacrificing, done hurting, done being the adult and the one expected to quickly forgive and hold everything together. I look back in awe at how the Lord has protected me from myself and from the enemy over the years. How He brought beauty from ashes and how we actually did have seasons of real love and joy in our marriage. I just wish they'd been sustained and not so temporary.

From that season, the Lord brought us to a place of reconciliation and restoration, and we started making our marriage a priority. Every Thursday night we set aside a couple of hours to lock away together and get into the Word. Our marriage started getting stronger, love started to bloom again, and it seemed like our family was becoming more united and healthier. The problems come when we lose sight of what's really important and begin to neglect the significant little things for other, far lesser things.

I've had to repent many, many times over the years for the role I played, the bad attitudes I embraced and the doors I left open for the enemy. Like I said, I'm not perfect and I'm no expert but there's power in our testimony and I carry keys of freedom for others who find themselves on the roads I've already walked down. Today can be your day of liberation!!

Numbers 32:23 says, *"Be sure your sin will find you out"*. If you're living a double life, like Danny and I were at times, why not get it right, right now? God already sees and knows every single detail and here's your chance for a clean slate. He's calling you. If your life looks different behind closed doors than it does in public, it's time to let the light in and allow the Lord to come and change everything that's not of Him. Right now, your heart is beating so hard and fast.... it's the Spirit of the Almighty beaconing you to come to Him. To have the life and marriage you've desired to have, you must be right with God first and allow Him to make straight all the crooked paths.

If you have an alcohol or drug problem, illicit or legal, or any secret sin problem God can take it from you if you'll be honest and give it to Him. He took pot smoking, cigarettes, drinking, cussing and all kinds of nonsense out of my life and He doesn't love me any more than He loves you. Take a minute and talk to Him if that's you. He's right there and He wants you to be in right standing with Him and in your right mind. Perhaps it's not about an act of sin but your thought life that condemns you. Now is the moment to set all that's wrong right.

Father, I lift the one reading this before You, who's coming to You for full freedom. I speak freedom from the shackles of addiction, guilt, shame, and condemnation, In Jesus name!! Be loosed now and never bound again in the mighty name of Jesus!! Freedom and healing over your mind, body, and spirit. New life, protection, healing and abundance over you, your marriage, and your family in Jesus' name!! Be filled with the Spirit of God, NOW! Be baptized with the Holy Spirit and Fire NOW, in Jesus' name!! Father, give them a hunger for your Word, order their steps and enable them to run their race and finish well. I thank you that they have it now. In Jesus' name!!

Glory to God!!!

If you just gave those things to the Lord, you don't EVER have to carry those burdens again. If you repented (acknowledged your sin and turned from it) and asked the Lord to forgive you, He is faithful to not only forgive you but to remember those things no more. Your account has been wiped clean!!

Jesus!!!

He's so very, very good!! Now go and sin no more. Don't pick those things back up. Share with someone you trust what you just did and allow them to help you stay accountable and stay free. Today is the first day of the rest of your life!! Praise the Lord!!!

And Danny, he's cheering you on from the banisters of heaven as you walk in the freedom he longed for this side of heaven. Don't take it lightly, don't get distracted. Stay the course and allow the Lord to unveil your God given destiny into the most wonderful life you've ever dreamt of having. Walking transparently in the presence of The King is the grandest adventure you'll ever embark on this side of heaven.

Key Takeaways

- Set healthy boundaries to protect your marriage.

- Be honest and transparent with yourself, your spouse & God.

- Prayerfully find an accountability partner and stay transparent & submitted to them.

Declarations:

❖ **According to Philippians 4:13, I can do all things through Christ who strengthens me.**

("I have strength for all things in Christ Who empowers me [I am ready for anything and equal to anything through Him Who infuses inner strength into me; I am self-sufficient in Christ's sufficiency].")

❖ **According to Romans 8:37, I am more than a conqueror through Christ Jesus.**

("Yet in all these things we are more than conquerors through Him who loved us.")

❖ **According to 1 John 4:4, I am an overcomer because the One who lives in me is greater than the one who is in the world.**

("Ye are of God, little children, and have overcome them: because greater is he that is in you, than he that is in the world.")

Chapter 8

Guard Your Heart

"Keep and guard your heart with all vigilance and above all that you guard, for out of it flow the springs of life. Put away from you false and dishonest speech, and willful and contrary talk put far from you. Let your eyes look right on [with fixed purpose], and let your gaze be straight before you. Consider well the path of your feet, and let all your ways be established and ordered aright. Turn not aside to the right hand or to the left; remove your foot from evil." Proverbs 4:23-27

I've heard it said many times, "show me the five people you're closest to and I'll show you your future". Not sure who can be originally credited with that phrase, but I've certainly found it to be true. We become like those we hang out with. For good or bad those we spend the most time with influence us and we influence them.

If we want to be godly wives and mothers, then we can't be spending much time with someone who doesn't respect and honor her husband or doesn't take good care of her children or home. Just as a godly man and husband can't hang out with worldly friends and expect to remain godly in all their dealings. It just doesn't work that way. It's kind of like drinking just a little poison every day and expecting it not to impact us. The fact of the matter is, it's still poison. It's just killing a person slower, and likely without them even knowing, simply because of the lesser amount. The end result, certain death, is the same though. So, it is when we entertain people, media or outside influences that run contrary to the Word of God and how He admonishes us to live.

This is an area where many struggle because it feels almost ungodly to pull away from someone, especially when they seem needy, they're family or we deeply care about them. Unfortunately, many are not interested in doing the work necessary to have a Christ centered marriage and family. But it's the straight and narrow path that's required to succeed in every area of life, especially when it comes to relationships.

I couldn't tell you how many relationships I've either had to walk away from or seen end abruptly because the Lord removed them from my life or revealed to me that they couldn't go where He was taking me. I choose to live a consecrated life before God. Does that mean I do it perfectly, of course not. But what it does mean is that I hold every relationship loosely before The King and give Him full access to every area of my life. And when He shows me something that needs to change or go, I submit.

We must come to trust that He knows things we don't. He hears conversations we don't, and He knows what's on the road ahead. We can trust Him to move things around as He sees fit but most often, He'll talk to us about dealing with it. He's not going to force His will. Perhaps you're being reminded of a relationship or connection that He's been talking to you about cutting off or pulling back from. Perhaps it's a show, some type of music or even a behavior. I encourage you to simply trust and obey. He would never call you to do something to hurt you, quite the opposite in fact. He's working everything out for your good. And if He's calling you to pull back or cut something off, He'll even show you how if you'll ask Him.

Many years ago, I had a friendship that was very much like a sister in my heart. She was single and didn't really have a paradigm for what marriage and being a mom required. I couldn't just come and go as I pleased, as she could. Regardless of anything else, our marriages and families must be first, second only to God. There was a lot of tension that grew in our friendship because we were in such different places in life, especially after Danny and I had some real breakthrough in our marriage and started spending more intentional time together. Over time the Lord removed that friendship.

I was broken hearted, but He showed me that she couldn't go with me where He was taking me. And I probably couldn't go with her any further on her journey either. There wasn't really any distinct event that ended our friendship, but it was obviously the Lord's will. It was a difficult reality and we'd tried to reconcile but it was just never the same. I bless her and I've prayed for her over the years, but I had to wrestle and come to terms with the fact that our friendship had to end.

When the Lord removes someone or shows you not to get close to them it's not always because they aren't saved or they're a bad person. Sometimes they just have bad habits, mindsets or behaviors that you shouldn't be influenced by. Sometimes it's that our partnering would hinder one or both of us and/or our families. If we spend time with someone who's always talking bad about their husband, has a poverty mindset, or any of the other many issues people struggle with, it will influence us. Do we love them? Of course. But if they aren't willing to work through those things with the Lord, are unwilling to acknowledge the issues or are satisfied with staying that way. They likely won't be someone you can really run with. They could even impede your growth and ability to really soar.

Years ago, I heard a story about a farmer that had a mysterious egg show up in his turkey coop. He protected it and after it hatched that bird didn't look much like those turkeys at all. A traveling man came by and saw the bird and inquired of the farmer. The farmer was frustrated as the bird didn't even act like those turkeys, but it was eating up the food and kept trying to fly out of the coop, hitting its head on the fencing above.

The stranger shed some light on the subject because that bird wasn't a turkey at all. And even though it tried to act like those it was surrounded by, it'd never be like them. That strange bird was actually an eagle. Eagles are meant for great heights not limitations. And you my dear, are called to be an eagle not a turkey. Turkeys can't teach an eagle how to fly and no matter how bad they want to; they're limited in their own God given ability. Turkeys have their own important roles to play but the fact of the matter is, they aren't eagles and they never will be.

So be careful who you keep company with and who you let have access to your heart. The people you spend the most time with are influencing you more than you know, that's precisely why we need to spend much time with Jesus. Then we can become like Him and bring His love to the world that's hurting around us. The only way we'll ever soar into the heights we're destined for is to spend time with Jesus and other eagles. And the only way to truly become who God created you to be is to accept Jesus and follow His leading as Lord of your life. That brings us to one of my favorite scriptures: *"But they that wait upon the LORD shall renew their strength; they shall mount up with wings as eagles; they shall run, and not be weary; and they shall walk, and not faint."* Isaiah 40:31

Outside Influencers

Now this topic may step on some toes, but I challenge you not to pull back. You've made it this far because you're serious about your marriage, your family and your walk with God. What some ministers won't tell you is how great of an influence tv, movies, music, etc. are on us personally but especially when it comes to our faith walk. These areas are a huge window that many churches have left wide open and unguarded, and it's left the body of Christ vulnerable to all sorts of nonsense and compromise.

Many people don't understand why a woman who's being beaten would stay. The unfortunate psychology behind it, however, is that their abuser typically shifts their beliefs little by little until they believe they deserve what they're getting. The result is that they begin to acclimate to the abuse and to change personally to accommodate their perceived, unavoidable reality. And while that perception isn't based on truth because of repetition and familiarity, they stay in that bondage.

I was in a very abusive relationship when I was 18, so I know this from personal experience. The physical abuse didn't start until after he'd told me again and again and again how unlovable, unwanted, and unworthy I was. Unfortunately, I started to believe those lies. I even believed that no one else would ever want me and I basically had to settle for whatever I was getting. The truth is if you hear something over and over you start to believe it, even if it's not true. We must be very intentional about what we allow to influence us, our marriages, and families. We must guard our hearts and protect what is sacred to us.

If you watch shows and movies that have promiscuity, adultery, demonic activity, drugs/drinking, cussing, pornography, homosexuality, sexting, abortion, etc. over time you'll become numb to those things and won't see anything wrong with them. The Bible makes it VERY CLEAR where God stands and where He says we should stand on those issues. So, we must choose, who are we going to live for?

As we saw at the beginning of this chapter, Proverbs 4:23-27 says, *"Keep and guard your heart with all vigilance and above all that you guard, for out of it flow the springs of life. Put away from you false and dishonest speech, and willful and contrary talk put far from you. Let your eyes look right on [with fixed purpose], and let your gaze be straight before you. Consider well the path of your feet, and let all your ways be established and ordered aright. Turn not aside to the right hand or to the left; remove your foot from evil."*

When you boil it all down, if God says it's sin, IT'S SIN! Period. No discussion required and no other opinions necessary. He is our Father and Creator and He's the only One who gets to say because He's the boss, Applesauce. Now we don't shun people who've been caught in the snares of sin, but we don't condone it either. And we certainly can't allow it to be prevalent in our own homes and families.

Matthew 5:27-30 makes the matter very clear, *"Ye have heard that it was said by them of old time, Thou shalt not commit adultery: But I say unto you, That whosoever looketh on a woman to lust after her hath committed adultery with her already in his heart. And if thy right eye offend thee, pluck it out, and cast it from thee: for it is profitable for thee that one of thy members should perish, and not that thy whole body should be cast into hell. And if thy right hand offend thee, cut it off, and cast it from thee: for it is profitable for thee that one of thy members should perish, and not that thy whole body should be cast into hell."*

We need to start treating sin like the deadly enemy that it really is. Just a little over time can lead to massive compromise and even backsliding all the way to hell. James 14:17 says, *"Therefore to him that knoweth to do good, and doeth it not, to him it is sin."* Making room for sin and ignoring the truth will not be justification for compromise when we stand before God and it will leave us, our marriages, and our families vulnerable.

If there's some area(s) of compromise that just came to mind, why not do something to change it? You decide. Even if your spouse isn't completely on the same page, you decide how you will walk and how great of an influence you'll have. Following blindly when we know things are against the Word or against God still makes us an accomplice. And we are just as accountable for the fruit of it.

No amount of temporary pleasure is worth missing heaven and people are watching, especially if you have children. They are learning far more from what you do and how you live than anything you say. Can you say as Paul did in 1Cor. 11:1, *"Be ye followers of me, even as I also am of Christ"*? I am working with the Lord daily to walk in such a way that this can be said of me. It's a personal, daily decision to pick up our cross and follow Jesus.

My prayer is that the Lord will reveal and continue to reveal to all of us if there are any areas of compromise and that we'll have the courage to close any breach. That we'll have wisdom beyond our years and that God will give us direction on the paths we need to take and the relationships we need to foster as well as the ones we need to let go of. In Jesus name!

The bible says the steps of the righteous are ordered of the Lord and I believe He's ordering your steps right now and even more everyday as you set your resolve to really follow Him and walk uprightly in all your ways. May He richly bless you in every single area of life!

Key Takeaways

- Who you hang out with matters, choose wisely.

- Trust God with the matters of the heart and shift where needed.

- Anything that's in the way of your walk with the Lord needs to be put in its proper place or it has to go.

Declarations:

❖ According to Proverbs 4:23, I will guard my heart above all else.

("Keep thy heart with all diligence; for out of it are the issues of life.")

❖ According to Psalm 37:23, My steps are ordered by the Lord.

("The steps of a good man are ordered by the Lord: and he delighteth in his way.")

❖ According to Isaiah 40:31, my strength is renewed, and I mount up on wings like an eagle. I run and don't grow weary; I walk and don't faint.

("But they that wait upon the LORD shall renew their strength; they shall mount up with wings as eagles; they shall run, and not be weary; and they shall walk, and not faint." Isaiah 40:31)

Chapter 9

Father Knows Best

All throughout this book I've been praying for you to find your way to really connect with God's sovereign plan for you, your marriage & family. The thing that I've learned the most as I've walked with the Lord is that Father does, indeed, know best. He knows how you're hardwired, what makes your heart sing. He knows how you're wired to communicate, to give and receive love. He knows best and He knows how to give you what's best for you.

If you seek His will above all else, He really will give you the desires of your heart. (Psalm 37:4) *"I love you lavishly. There will be times and things in your heart, things that you desire that your spouse won't be equipped to meet. Only one can fulfill some of those longings in the depths of your soul."* As you turn to God, and you give him your heart aches, you're honest and open with him and as you seek Him first, He'll give you that fulfillment. In the dark of night, even if your spouse feels 1,000 miles away, you can turn to Him. You can turn to God, and He will answer you.

His Word says, *"draw near to me and I will draw near to you"*, James 4:8. His Word is true, and He is not a man that He should lie so He will, and He does indeed draw near as we do. In the loneliness you can cry out, in the frustration, He's right there. The word says that He's near to the broken and contrite. (Psalm 34:18) And I've so found that to be true after all these years and throughout the ebbs and flows of life. I've found Him to be my husband everywhere my earthly husband lacked and all the more today. He truly is the husband to the widow.

I've also found Him to be the Father to the fatherless. And I don't believe that just means for orphans. I believe that means for anywhere a person is orphaned, or their parental figures lack. He wants to fill in the gap. In fact, there were countless times when He gave me wisdom on raising or disciplining my kids. He'd even reveal to me where things were or if someone was lying.

We find our fulfillment in God, not in a person and certainly not with the one in the mirror. We find our total fulfillment in Him alone. And that's actually what eternity will be all about, to know God, to really know Him and be intimately acquainted with Him.

We're supposed to have heaven on earth, this side of heaven. To be conduits of His grace, mercy, and love to all those we encounter. But to know Him, to press into the Lord God Almighty. And to come to know His ways. To dive deep into the Word and allow it to change us and become a part of who we are but not just in part. That we would purely, more rightly, represent who He is. In John 1:1 again says, *"In the beginning was the Word. The Word was with God and the Word was God"*. And the word became flesh and He dwelt among us. We're to be so filled with the Word that we begin to look, act, and talk like the Lord, who is The Word who became flesh.

To become so saturated in the word that we truly can be living epistles read of men as Paul admonishes in 2 Corinthians 3:2. That our marriages would exemplify the love of Jesus. That our lives would be examples of His love. *"Perfect love casts out fear."* 1 John 4:18 Perfect love. God is perfect love and the more we become like Him the more fear will be gone. It'll be broken off of us individually, off our marriages, and off our families. And He will be glorified! He will be the One that gets the glory from our marriages and from our families. From the way we raise our kids to the way we interact with strangers. The way we do business and handle our relationships. And the more we do it to glorify Him, the more He's honored, and people will be drawn to Him.

Recently I was listening to a class, and the instructor was talking about how Jesus, when He was heading to that cross, love was His motivator. In the word it talks about how He kept going because of the joy that was set before Him. (Hebrews 12:2) Do you realize… You were that joy? You were the joy set before Him. What kept Him going, what kept Him hanging on that cross. He could've easily gotten down. He could've called down a thousand angels and said, "forget it, I'm not doing it".

But He didn't. Oh, am I glad He didn't!!!

He didn't, He willingly hung there. He chose to hang there as our atoning sacrifice. Yet so often we get offended by people and we shut the door on them, we walk away. We must learn to love like Jesus. I'm not talking about the relationships He calls us to walk away from now, I'm referring to the day-to-day interaction. The ones He has brought into our lives.

In order for our marriages to work we must walk in and be motivated by love. Truly becoming vessels of love, looking more like the King Himself. Let us be transformed by the renewing of our minds and may we never grow weary in doing well. May we love them well and learn to love ourselves well. May we honor the King and be examples for the world to see. *"By this shall all men know that ye are my disciples, if ye have love one to another."* John 13:35

"Three things will last forever—faith, hope, and love—and the greatest of these is love." 1 Corinthians 13:13 We must have faith that God will answer our prayers and that He's faithful to His Word. In fact, without faith, it's impossible to even please Him. (Hebrews 11:6) We must have hope for a future that's far greater than our past and we must learn to love, to truly love. For it is one of the most powerful forces on earth.

The Lord wants to give us instructions every day. The Word says that the steps of the righteous are ordered of Him. So, if you're a son or daughter of the Most High God, Jesus has made you righteous and He loves to give you direction. Direction for your marriage, finances, raising your kids and having healthy relationships. Managing your home, business and really every area of life. He wants to help you and be with you.

His desire hasn't changed from the garden in Genesis. His desire is still to daily commune with man and walk with His beloved.

To love you lavishly and fill your cup to overflow. To fill you up to such great a measure that everyone gets splashed on that comes into close proximity. That's how we overcome the darkness.

That's how we overcome insecurities, disappointments and hope deferred. Perfect love will cast out all fear. God Himself is the only true solution, and He sent His Holy Spirit to walk with us every step of the way. He's the One that gave me the staying power in my marriage. Glory! Glory to the Lord Most High!

A Sacred Covenant

May Christian marriages, across the world, begin to really look like Him and become as He originally intended marriage to be in the garden. May people that claim to be Christians really begin to represent our Father in holiness, righteousness, and purity. Christian means Christ like one. May we be that, may we begin to represent Him rightly in every area of life, to really look like our King. Not merely give lip service, wear some religious badge or have a fish on our car. But have a real, tangible relationship with the Sovereign, Triune God. That's what it takes. And it's so worth it! He will fulfill us on every level. He's the only One that can. And He is faithful to finish ALL that He begins.

If you entered into a covenant before God Almighty, you can trust Him to help you do whatever it takes to walk that out even if it's less than ideal. You really can trust HIM. He was there on that day you made those vows. He was there and He takes it very seriously. He wants to enable and empower you & your spouse to be able to stand the test of time and really walk out and honor that God ordained covenant. To be able to see it through. No matter how hard it's been, no matter what challenges have come.

He wants you to fight for your marriage, to fight for your family. LOVE is worth fighting for. Now you don't have to set your sights on lofty goals and things that feel unattainable, just tackle today, even just this next 5 minutes if it's come to that. His grace will meet you where you're at. Set out to make God the Lord of your life, your marriage, and your home. Why not take a moment and invite Him to be that third strand in the cord of your marriage if He hasn't held that place? *"And if one prevail against him, two shall withstand him; and a threefold cord is not quickly broken."*, Ecclesiastes 4:12. Why not prayerfully acknowledge Him as a couple, repent where necessary and start today with a clean slate before God and with each other, if needed?

Sometimes we get off balance by allowing something or someone else to take up residence on the throne of our hearts. God's a jealous God and that's a place fit only for Him, and it should be reserved for Him alone, He's the only One that can properly be seated there anyway. So, let's kick out any idols that have taken that position in our hearts and invite the Lord to come in and take His rightful place again. To fully be Lord of our lives.

Every other relationship will flow from that. They'll come into proper alignment with the King. Proper alignment with heaven. With what we're designed for, Jesus is the answer. Jesus has always been the answer. He's been the answer from before the beginning of time. God knew we would need an answer, we would need a solution to our self-imposed separation from Him, our sin problem. He knew we would desperately need a Savior. And He willingly sent His son, the spotless and holy One to die in our place.

The day that Jesus died the veil was torn that separated us. (See Matthew 27:50-51) That veil was torn for all of humanity so He could come and dwell IN us and have restored fellowship with us. The enemy overplayed his hand on the day Jesus died. Because what really happened was a way was made for God Himself to live inside of mankind like never before, hence multiplying His presence in physical form on earth. In Him we live and move and have our being. (Acts 17:28) He's the One. The risen Son. And He's still the answer to all of humanity's problems today.

The Grand Master

On Pentecost Sunday of 2020, I was at The Stand at the River of Tampa Bay Church, with a friend. I got so filled with the fire of God in those first three days that I was prophesying and experiencing the supernatural in ways I hadn't expected. On our way home we stopped at my brother's house in Saint Charles and had a little revival style meeting there. My youngest nephew received some amazing healing, and it was a truly powerful time. We got back to Lawson, Mo. that Thursday. On that trip the Lord had been talking to me about my marriage and how it wasn't enough just to "white knuckle it" and honor my covenant but I needed to keep my heart soft toward him. No matter what he was or wasn't doing. So, I set out to do just that.

When I got home on Thursday I was immediately tested as my house was a mess. I prayed, held my tongue, and cleaned it up. We were able to reconnect Friday night and even went to our youngest son's house Saturday for some family time. When Sunday morning rolled around Danny had the "Sunday Bug". You know the kind where everything seems ok until it's time for church. This is the way it was for much of our marriage, so I didn't think too much of it. He had mentioned not feeling great while I was out of town but that too wasn't too out of the ordinary.

He said, "I think I'm just gonna stay home". I said, "you could do that, or you could come to church and get healed". He didn't want to go. The Holy Spirit prompted me to pray the fire of God into Him, so I leaned in, put my hand on his chest and quietly prayed the fire of God into him. He said, "what did you say?". I said, "the fire of God that's what I brought home with me". He said, "I don't feel so good". I told him to let the Lord have his way with him that he'd be just fine.

In my spirit I was all lit up. I knew dark and light were colliding, and God was about to win REALLY BIG!! I kissed him goodbye, and my daughters and I went on to church. We had a holy ghost good time that Sunday. Nothing out of the ordinary, just a powerful morning. We didn't hear from him but that wasn't unusual when he'd gotten out of going with us, he'd usually just lay low for the day.

When my youngest daughter and I got back home that evening we could feel something was off in the driveway. When we went up the stairs she went straight outside, and I found his lifeless body. As I stood over him, I knew I carried the power that raised Lazarus from the dead and if I commanded him to raise, he would. But the Lord slowed me, way, down. He basically told me I could command him to raise, and he would, or I could defer to the will of God. So, I commanded him to raise if it were the will of God but ultimately deferred to Him. He didn't raise.

That night I felt the wind of the Spirit and the Lord said, "he's up here with Me". It was in those few words that I felt the Lord saying, "Drop your armor baby. You don't have to battle one more day on his behalf. No more fasting, no more praying, no more contending. The battle has been won!" GLORY TO GOD!!! Later the Lord showed me, had he been raised that day he would've ended up in hell because of the choices he was and would continue making. When I prayed the fire into him it burned up all the strongholds and shackles of the enemy so Danny could choose one more time, JESUS.

You see the enemy was so sure he had him, BUT GOD!!! God is the Master chess player, the Grand Master if you will, and the enemy always overplays his hand. At Danny's celebration of life service six people gave their lives to the Lord!! Now was it God's perfect will for Danny to die at 47? Of course not! But in His mercy, grace, and infinite wisdom He made a way where it seemed like there was no way. Because of ignorance, on Danny's part, he was heading into eternity on June 7, 2020, for heaven or hell. But God saw fit to secure his place with Him for all of eternity. And God alone gets the glory, honor, and praise for that. I will forever be grateful for the hand of God in his life and on our family through all of this.

Now I certainly didn't share that to make you fearful of the fire of God, though people living in blatant sin probably should be. As children of the Most High God, we should welcome the fire of God because our God is a consuming fire according to Hebrews 12:29, the fire is really Him. And Jesus is the great baptizer of the holy spirit and fire according to Luke 3:16 & Matthew 3:11. We'll go more into that in the next chapter but bear in mind that God has not given us a spirit of fear but of power, love, and a sound mind according to 2 Timothy 1:7.

Key Takeaways

- God can make a way, even in seemingly impossible situations. He is the Master chess player!

- Marriage is a covenant established by God, and He will enable us to honor and keep our vows. Divorce is not His perfect will.

- The Lord wants to walk with us through every season of life.

Declarations:

❖ **According to Ephesians 3:20-21, my God is able to do exceedingly, abundantly above all I ask or think according to the power that is working in me.**

("Now unto him that is able to do exceedingly abundantly above all that we ask or think, according to the power that worketh in us, Unto him be glory in the church by Christ Jesus throughout all ages, world without end. Amen." Ephesians 3:20-21)

❖ **According to Jeremiah 29:11, God's thoughts towards me are of welfare and peace and not evil. And He plans to give me hope for my future.**

("For I know the thoughts and plans that I have for you, says the Lord, thoughts and plans for welfare and peace and not for evil, to give you hope in your final outcome.")

❖ **According to 1 John 4:7-8, God is love and since I am born of God, I love well, and I know God.**

("Beloved, let us love one another: for love is of God; and everyone that loveth is born of God, and knoweth God. He that loveth not knoweth not God; for God is love. 1 John 4:7-8")

Chapter 10

Holy Spirit & Fire

"John answered, saying unto them all, I indeed baptize you with water; but one mightier than I cometh, the latchet of whose shoes I am not worthy to unloose: he shall baptize you with the Holy Ghost and with fire: Whose fan is in his hand, and he will throughly purge his floor, and will gather the wheat into his garner; but the chaff he will burn with fire unquenchable." Luke 3:16-17

In this passage we see that Jesus is indeed the One who baptizes in the Holy Ghost & Fire. Fire has many distinct purposes and qualities. For instance, under metal it refines but a wildfire devours. The impact of each one is vastly different from the other yet they're both still fire. The fire of God works similarly. There's much to learn about the fire of God, His ways are much higher than ours and we're always learning and growing if we're truly following Him.

I'm still learning about the baptism of fire and the God who answers by fire, and I will be for the rest of my days. But I am called to share with you what I do know and what I've freely received I give unto you. I can tell you that I personally received that baptism of fire in December of '18. And it changed everything! I was baptized in the

Holy Spirit in '02 but had since longed for the fire. I believe that both were received on the day of Pentecost but for some reason it seems that's not the case in many believers lives today. Or perhaps believers haven't been taught enough about the fullness of what they've received so they don't see the full manifestation of what's available. Either way the church needs the Holy Spirit & Fire that Jesus baptizes with.

There are many Spirit-filled believers that have never experienced the fire of God and certainly don't appear to have received the Baptism of Fire spoken of in Luke 3:16. Now I don't believe that it was ever God's plan for His kids to go without but so often we restrict the Lord on how much access we give Him and how much we're willing to receive. Far too often we block off areas in our own lives and set up no trespassing signs where the Lord isn't allowed to go. Other times we are limited in our doctrine, deep rooted beliefs, and lack of faith on just how big and who He really is. If we could just grab ahold of the fact that His plans for us are good and He'll never do anything towards us that's evil. And unlike mere men, He can be fully trusted. It would change everything. We need the baptism of the Holy Spirit & Fire.

Bad doctrine can greatly keep us from receiving the fullness of His will. We must become a people of the Word that refuse to accept anything contrary to His Word. No matter how much we respect our leaders we must compare what they say to the Word and only accept what is confirmed by the sovereign word of God, even if no one else adheres to it. We must fully embrace the fact that, *"All scripture is given by inspiration of God, and is profitable for doctrine, for reproof, for correction, for instruction in righteousness: That the man of God may be perfect, throughly furnished unto all good works. "*, 2 Timothy 3:16. In Psalms 138:2 we see that God, Himself, even magnifies His Word above His own name. If the uncreated One regards His Word with such esteem how much more should the created?

Make no mistake, He honors our free will, He gave it to us and He's not retracting that even when it means some choose hell over eternity in heaven. The question is, will we be wise as serpents yet gentle as doves as we're admonished in Matthew 10:6? Will we choose to be a people that aren't limited by what we can understand with our finite minds in order to embrace the fullness of God's providential plan for our lives? Will we stir ourselves up to become hungry and thirsty for the more we see in scripture?

I fully acknowledge that that's why you're even reading my testimony among these pages and seeing the glorious intervention of God Almighty in my late marriage and my life. It's not because I'm something great or that I'm His favorite, though He sure makes me feel like it sometimes. He's the One that's great. And if we'll seek Him, we truly will find, if we knock the door will be opened and if we ask it will be given unto us. (Matthew 7:7-8)

I submit to you that the 120, the remnant that remained in that upper room on the day of Pentecost in Acts 2, were a hungry bunch. They weren't interested in getting just a little of what Jesus said would come. They wanted it ALL! We too must get hungry like that. We NEED the Holy Spirit and the Fire! We need the touch of God!!! And not just once. There's one baptism but many in-fillings.

I received the baptism of the Holy Spirit, with evidence of speaking in tongues, the Thursday before Easter in '02. I'd been to some meetings where people were praying to receive the baptism but didn't personally get it, so I got desperate. I was pressing into the

Lord, kneeled beside my bed, just praying, and worshiping Him. When suddenly, strange sounds started coming out of my mouth. My mind & the enemy tried to make me believe it was just gibberish, but I knew better. I kept praying and pressing in and before I knew it a heavenly language was rolling out of my mouth. Glory to God!!

Not that I worked for it, not at all. We can't earn or manufacture the things of God, we need only believe and receive. But I stayed focused on the Lord and gave Him access and permission to move through me as He saw fit. What started out as sounds of a child babbling and learning to talk became a bubbling brook and a rushing river and now, I even sing in the Spirit. And the beautiful thing is we'll never exhaust the infinite wonder and splendor of the King, nor of His ways.

If you've been baptized in the Holy Spirit, you need to be praying in the Spirit daily. Do you realize that when you do, you're actually praying the perfect will of God? That's so important and a total game changer. If you've not received the Baptism of the Holy Spirit but desire to, you first need to know that it's a gift from God and it is His will that you would have it. So, all you need to do is ask

Jesus to baptize you and believe that if you ask anything according to His will that you will have it. (1 John 5:14-15)

If that's you, and you've never received the baptism, or it's been a long time since you've spoken in tongues and allowed the rivers to flow let's talk to the Lord about it right now. Say with me out loud and from your heart: "Dear Lord Jesus, forgive me of my sins both known and unknown. Be my Lord and be my Savior. Make me a vessel that's clean and pure, prepared for holy use. Jesus, Your Word says You are the baptizer of the Holy Ghost and Fire and I want all you have for me. Lord, please baptize me now, in your Holy name. I thank you that I have it now! Amen!"

Now start to worship and pray out loud from your heart and allow Him to flow through you. Be baptized NOW, in Jesus' name!!

The Holy Spirit and praying in tongues have helped me through the last 20 plus years of my walk with the Lord. When you don't know how to pray or when it's hard to pray for someone who hurts you, pray in tongues. When you need wisdom, direction, peace, anything… pray in the Spirit. He is our comforter according to John 14:26; Our seal of Redemption according to Ephesians 4:30; He empowers us to walk according to the Word and righteousness according to Ezekiel 36:27; He'll even give us the very words to speak according to Mark 13:11 and so much more!! We need Him and we need to learn to work with Him.

Relentless Pursuit

When you read of me praying the fire of God into Danny in chapter 9 perhaps you had questions, maybe fear tried to rise up or maybe you had no idea there even was such a thing. We'll build as we go but I want to share some of my personal journey with you.

Sometime during '18, I believe, I was reading in Mark 16:15-18 where it says, *"And he said unto them, Go ye into all the world, and preach the gospel to every creature. He that believeth and is baptized shall be saved; but he that believeth not shall be damned. And these signs shall follow them that believe; In my name shall they cast out devils; they shall speak with new tongues; They shall take up serpents; and if they drink any deadly thing, it shall not hurt them; they shall lay hands on the sick, and they shall recover."*

The last part really struck me. Why weren't we seeing devils coming out and the sick being healed regularly when we lay hands on them. And then in John 14:12 where Jesus said, *"Verily, verily, I say unto you, He that believeth on me, the works that I do shall he do also; and greater works than these shall he do, because I go unto my Father"*. How in the world are we to do greater things than Jesus did? Us doing those greater works that our Savior spoke of are tied directly to believing in Him, receiving the One He sent and the baptism of Holy Spirit and Fire that endues us with power.

I got so hungry; it became my heart's cry to have the more that I'd been reading about. And in December of '18, at the Jesus Conference in Orlando, I had encounters with the Holy Spirit that I had no paradigm for. It was like the day of Pentecost on blast. People were laid out everywhere under the power, filled with joy and looking drunk like we read of in Acts 2. Deliverance, healings, and baptisms in the Spirit were popping like popcorn. It was unreal, I could hardly believe what I was seeing let alone what I was personally experiencing.

The Lord had plans to change my whole life that week and boy did He! Multiple times at those meetings I had fire all over me and I got slain in the spirit and filled with the joy of the Lord more times than I can count. The last night of the conference I was still desperate for more. The more I tasted of Him and His glorious presence, the hungrier I got. I was already under the power of God and could hardly get out of my chair, let alone walk. But when the minister said if anyone wants more of God come down front, I begged the ones around me to help me go forward. In no time at all I was back on the floor with heated contractions surging through my body.

I was crying out "Lord kill me until it's only You who lives through me", "wear me like a glove like you did Gideon". I was stuck to that floor for about two hours. I had to be helped to my seat and still had difficulty walking when I was leaving. I was getting what I'd been crying out for, it marked me and from there on everything began to change. One touch.... even just one touch can change everything.

When I got back to the church I was in leadership at, I started seeing people get miraculously healed or slain in the Spirit when I'd pray for them. I was falling back in love with my King in new ways and the Word started opening up in the most glorious fashion. It was like reading the Word for the first time. Secular work became very empty as I knew I was called to and schooled for ministry. My personal time with the Lord started to bloom in the most beautiful ways and I started prophesying like I never had before. I'd come back a very different woman.

Church per the norm was bland and empty. People started getting nervous as they watched the power of God moving on and through me. Often the Lord would give me a word for the church or people in particular, and my prayer life took on a new fiery boldness that sometimes even scared me. Conviction, repentance, healings, and prophecy were increasing in the church. But there were some who didn't care for what the Lord was doing. Personally, I just wanted Him to move, no matter what it looked like. Eventually I stepped down and left that church, per the Lord's leading, to press deeper into Him and focus more on my marriage and family.

The supernatural things of God began to open up to me and I saw a marked increase in visions, dreams and the prophetic. I wanted everyone to receive what I'd found but my words fell short. And unfortunately, many people aren't actually interested in fully yielding to the Holy Spirit. They start getting nervous because He's unpredictable and we are no longer the ones in control, we must surrender our control to His. He's not at all interested in staying within the confines of an hour-long service nor within the box of man's religion. He's looking for a people who will dare to take Him at His Word and step out into the great unknown to see the supernatural ways of God. Make no mistake, the fire will cost you. The anointing will cost you.

On that fateful day of June 7th, '20, when I prayed the fire into Danny, I didn't know what to expect. I didn't know what would happen or what God would do. But I knew my God. Because He's shown me who He is, how very good He is. I've come to trust Him with childlike faith. Not that I've arrived, I'm still growing in my faith. But I knew enough about my God to trust that if He was prompting me to pray fire into Danny then He had a plan.

Later the Lord showed me that when I prayed the fire into him, all the strongholds of the enemy, all the bondage he kept stepping back into was burned up in an instant and he was set free. Gloriously and completely free!! For that brief moment in time, he was set completely free from all demonic oppression so he could choose, one more time, JESUS!

Some mistakenly think that the fire that went into him that day killed him but that couldn't be further from the truth. It liberated him!!! Throughout Danny's life he'd wrestled with addictions, mindsets and unforgiveness that held him in bondage. He would press into the Lord and get free but over time he'd wander back into those shackles that were oh so familiar. Each time a person does that it gets harder and harder to get and stay free.

We cannot afford to play with sin. We cannot dance with the devil and expect to stay free. It's a trap!! But the fire of God burns those things up so we can not only get free but stay free. We need the fire!! We need to be refined in order to draw nearer to the Holy One and to become all He has in His heart for us to become. We need all He has provided for us in order to live victoriously on this side of heaven.

In marriage and in parenting one of the best things we can ever learn to do is to entrust the ones we love into the faithful hands of the Father. To lift them before Him daily. To trust and yield to His transformative ways and to fully yield personally so He can have His way in us and through us. To go low and stay burning for the King, holding nothing back. This is the sure way to victory!

Key Takeaways

- We NEED the baptism of the Holy Spirit & Fire!

- Whatever God says to do, DO.

- Praying in the spirit builds us up and allows us to pray the perfect will of God.

Declarations:

❖ According to 1 John 5:14-15, I know that if I ask anything according to God's will, He hears me and if He hears me then I know I have the petitions that I desire.

("And this is the confidence that we have in him, that, if we ask any thing according to his will, he heareth us: And if we know that he hear us, whatsoever we ask, we know that we have the petitions that we desired of him.")

❖ According to Matthew 5:6, as I hunger and thirst for righteousness I shall be filled. And because I am hungry and thirsty, I am being filled NOW in Jesus name!

("Blessed are they which do hunger and thirst after righteousness: for they shall be filled.")

Letter From the Author

Dear Reader,

I pray as you seek to employ the tools you've acquired in this book that you're empowered to fight well. That you have the courage to stay & trust God no matter what comes your way and that you have the boldness and wisdom to intentionally alter the trajectory of your family for generations to come. I pray my testimonies and God given insights have helped you make any necessary adjustments and equipped you to build the future and marriage you've been longing for. The fact that you've been faithful to finish this book tells me that you not only take God's plans for you seriously, but you are poised to win!

May the One True God embolden, strengthen, encourage, and guide you every single step of your journey. And may many testimonies of His goodness and grace spring forth as you set out to fulfill ALL of heavens plans for your life.

If He's called you to it, He'll see you through it. In Jesus name!

Much love in Him,

Hope

Bibliography

Amplified Bible, Classic Edition (AMPC). (1987). *Lockman.*

Authorized king James Version. (KJV) (Thomas Nelson Bibles., Trans.). (1987).

The Oxford Pocket Dictionary of Current English.. (yoke). https://www.encyclopedia.com/humanities/dictionaries-thesauruses-pictures-and-press-releases/yoke-0.

Merriam-Webster. (n.d.). Guard. In Merriam-Webster.com dictionary. (n.d.).

About the Author

Rev. Hope Lundy is a licensed minister through RMIMA, under the covering of Drs. Rodney & Adonica Howard-Browne, she's ordained through Ascend Academy, under the covering of Brian Guerin and has a BA from Southwestern Assembly of God University, in Waxahachie, Texas.

She's a traveling, 5-fold minister, who's called to bring liberty to the captives, provoke deep and personal intimacy with The King and to equip the saints for the work of the ministry in preparation of the days ahead. She's served in leadership at a local church in Missouri for many years as well as serving other local and well-known ministries, for nearly 20 years. She was launched into full-time ministry in '22 after the homegoing of her late husband, Danny. Her God given, ministry's name is Ray of Hope Restoration, and her website & blog can be found at: www.RayofHopeRestoration.org.

Hope currently resides near Tampa, Florida with her youngest daughter. Though a native of Missouri God moved them to Tampa in the summer of '21 to prepare for the launch into full time international ministry. She's a young widow, mother of 4 and Gigi of 4 darling grandbabies. She's an avid learner and student of The Word who's always seeking to grow, go into deeper levels of consecration and to become all God intends her to be.

Danny & Hope Lundy were married on June 15th, 2002, and were together for nearly 18 years before his sudden, and unexpected departure into heaven on June 7, '20. Hope learned through many years of difficulties, disappointments, rejections and struggles how to fight well for, instead of with, her late husband & family. How to navigate and guard against bitterness and offense. And how to allow the Lord to not only have access to every area of her life but to order her steps and equip her to train others to do the same.

The multifaceted experiences, victories, and failures that Rev. Hope has had over the years, are now an asset to the body of Christ as she carries the anointing to break the yoke of bondage, the keys to liberate the captives and the presence & anointing of the Lord everywhere she goes. She is determined to point all to Jesus and bring Him much glory as she personally answers His call into the nations.

Contact Information:

Rev. Hope D. Lundy

Ministry Website & Blog: www.RayofHopeRestoration.org

Ministry Email: RayofHopeRestoration@gmail.com